PREFACE TO THE FIRST EDITION

For many years Ted Barrett's boo guided travellers on the Grand Ca has not only allowed us to make has also given us the benefit o preparing this guide.

We are also grateful to the follow Liam Foynes, John Gleeson, Reggie Goodbody, Hugh Gough (fishing notes), Robert Jobson, Paul Kerrigan, John McNamara and Michael Gill.

This Guide is dedicated to the Commodore of the Royal and Ancient Bog of Allen Yacht Club, Mr. Seamus Kelly.

October 1975

Ruth Delany
Jeremy Addis

PREFACE TO THE SIXTH EDITION

This edition of the *Guide to the Grand Canal* is based on earlier editions originally produced by the Inland Waterways Association of Ireland (IWAI). ***Dúchas* The Heritage Service** of the Department of Arts, Heritage, Gaeltacht and the Islands has now taken over responsibility for this publication, and is indebted to the IWAI for its invaluable work. In particular we would like to thank Ruth Delany for her tireless and painstaking efforts.

In addition to navigation notes, some new aspects are dealt with, to reflect the modern role of the canal, which is a multi-faceted one, incorporating many different recreational activities - boating, walking, fishing and nature appreciation. This wider amenity use which ***Dúchas* The Heritage Service** is encouraging is represented by a section on Ecology and Wildlife and by an expanded piece on fishing. In addition, maps and text have been included for the Naas-Corbally section and for the entire Kilbeggan Branch, to promote interest in these stretches where improvements are being carried out.

November 1999

***Dúchas* The Heritage Service**

CONTENTS:

by: ***Dúchas* The Heritage Service**, with the co-operation of the Inland Waterways Association of Ireland.

GENERAL INFORMATION

The Grand Canal is administered by ***Dúchas* The Heritage Service**, of the Department of Arts, Heritage, Gaeltacht and the Islands, 17 / 19 Lower Hatch Street, Dublin 2, tel. (01) 647 3000.

The Main Line of the canal crosses Leinster from Ringsend in Dublin City to the River Shannon at Shannon Harbour in Co. Offaly. It is 82 miles (131 km) long with 43 locks, 5 of which are doubles. There are in addition three sea-locks linking the Grand Canal Basin in Ringsend with the tidal River Liffey. The Barrow Line (28 miles/45 km and 9 locks, including 2 doubles) runs south from the summit level at Lowtown in Co. Kildare to join the River Barrow in Athy. The Naas Branch is navigable to Naas Harbour (2 miles/4 km with 5 single locks) but a low bridge blocks the navigation from there to the old harbour at Corbally, 5 miles (8 km) away. The Kilbeggan Branch has not been restored (it was closed to navigation in 1961, and became very overgrown in the intervening years). A walking path is being opened along this branch.

The numbering of the locks in Dublin can be confusing. The original canal terminus was James's Street Harbour, and a short length of canal (now filled in) led from there to Lock 1 at Kilmainham. The Circular Line and Ringsend Basin, although opened as long ago as 1796, came later. The seven locks on the Circular Line therefore had to be numbered separately, and so there are two sets of locks 1-7 in Dublin.

Speed

SPEED LIMIT:	4 mph; 6 km/h
LUAS TEORAINN:	4 mile san uair;6 cilimeadar san uair
HÖCHSTGESCHWINDIGKEIT:	6 km/h
LIMITATION DE VITESSE:	6 km/h
LIMITE DI VELOCITÀ:	6 km all'ora

Permits Permits for lock passage and mooring must be obtained from ***Dúchas* The Heritage Service** at 17 / 19 Lower Hatch Street, Dublin 2; or from the lock-keepers at Ringsend (tel. (01) 668 9466), 19th Lock (tel. (045) 860 237), or 35th Lock (tel. (0509) 51163). Charges: 50p per lock, £10 per month for mooring,£100 per annum for lock passage and mooring.

Dimensions Maximum dimensions of craft permitted to use the canal:

Length	61 ft	18.50 m
Beam	13 ft	3.90 m
Draft	4 ft	1.20 m
Height over water	9 ft	2.75 m

N.B. The two bridges over Ringsend Basin are the lowest on the system. General McMahon Bridge, dividing the inner and outer basins, has a clearance of 8ft 3in (2.48m) at normal water level, but can be raised if arrangements are made in advance with ***Dúchas* The Heritage Service.** The railway bridge has a clearance of 8ft 2in (2.45m) over a width of 10ft (3m). Draught over 3ft 6in (1.05m) is inadvisable in summer and in Dublin.

Traffic Keep to the right. Overtake, when safe, on the left.

Equipment Boats must show a name or number and a valid permit from ***Dúchas* The Heritage Service.** They must have sufficient crew to handle them effectively, a good stop rope, mooring lines, fenders and a boat hook. Two mooring hooks will be found useful, and a lock key (a crank with 1.25 in or 3 cm square hollow section) is essential because many lock-keepers do not live at the locks, and you may have to operate the gear yourself. Be careful to observe the correct locking procedure (page 55) and comply with the official bye-laws.

Navigation Navigation is not allowed between the hours of sunset and sunrise.

Locks in Dublin Some of the locks in the Dublin area have been modified for operational reasons. It is important to contact the local lock-keepers or ***Dúchas* The Heritage Service** to arrange passage through Dublin.

Moorings Do not tie up at locks or bridges so as to obstruct the navigation. Tail gate (deep gate) jetties are for the use of boats waiting to use the lock only.

Dry Dock Tullamore and Shannon Harbour (£11.00 per day). The dry dock in Athy is not operable at present (1999) but will be restored in the future. Boat yard with hauling-out facilities at Lowtown - Tel. (045) 860 427.

Slips Ringsend Basin, 9th Lock (Clondalkin), Robertstown, George's Bridge (Edenderry), Tullamore Harbour (office hours only), Rathangan, Monasterevin and Athy.

Fuel Marine diesel is available at only two places: Lowtown Marina and Celtic Canal Cruisers Base at 24th lock near Tullamore. Garages are marked on the maps where petrol (and road-taxed diesel in some cases) would be available. Plan your refuelling carefully. Containers of a comfortable size for carrying are useful.

Safety Lock chambers are not equipped with ladders or life-buoys. It is advisable to wear life-jackets in locks, particularly for non-swimmers.

Swimming Swimming is not allowed in any lock, harbour or dock. Never swim near a lock when the sluices are open. Boaters, look out for swimmers at all times.

Health The quality of the water is generally good but, unlike tap water, it is untreated and micro-organisms are naturally present. The risk of contracting illness (including Weil's Disease) is small, but you should take sensible precautions:

- cover any cuts with a waterproof dressing;
- wash with clean water after water-based activities;
- if you become ill within two weeks, let your doctor know that you have been in contact with untreated water.

Walking The towpath of the Main Line from Dublin to Shannon Harbour has been designated the Grand Canal Way. The towpath from Lowtown to Athy is to be developed as the Barrow Way, which will continue along the trackway of the Barrow Navigation to St. Mullins.

Dogs Dogs should be kept on a lead at all times.

Maps Ordnance Survey half-inch sheets numbers 15 &16. Ordnance Survey (Discovery Series) 1:50 000 sheets numbers 47, 48, 49, 50 & 55.

Further reading

Ireland's Inland Waterways by Ruth Delany, Appletree Press, revised edition 1993.

Green and Silver by L T C Rolt, 3rd edition Athlone Branch IWAI, 1993.

The Grand Canal of Ireland by Ruth Delany, 2nd edition - Waterways Service / Lilliput Press 1995.

The Grand Canal in Inchicore & Kilmainham by Inchicore & Kilmainham Development Project, 2nd edition - OPW, 1994.

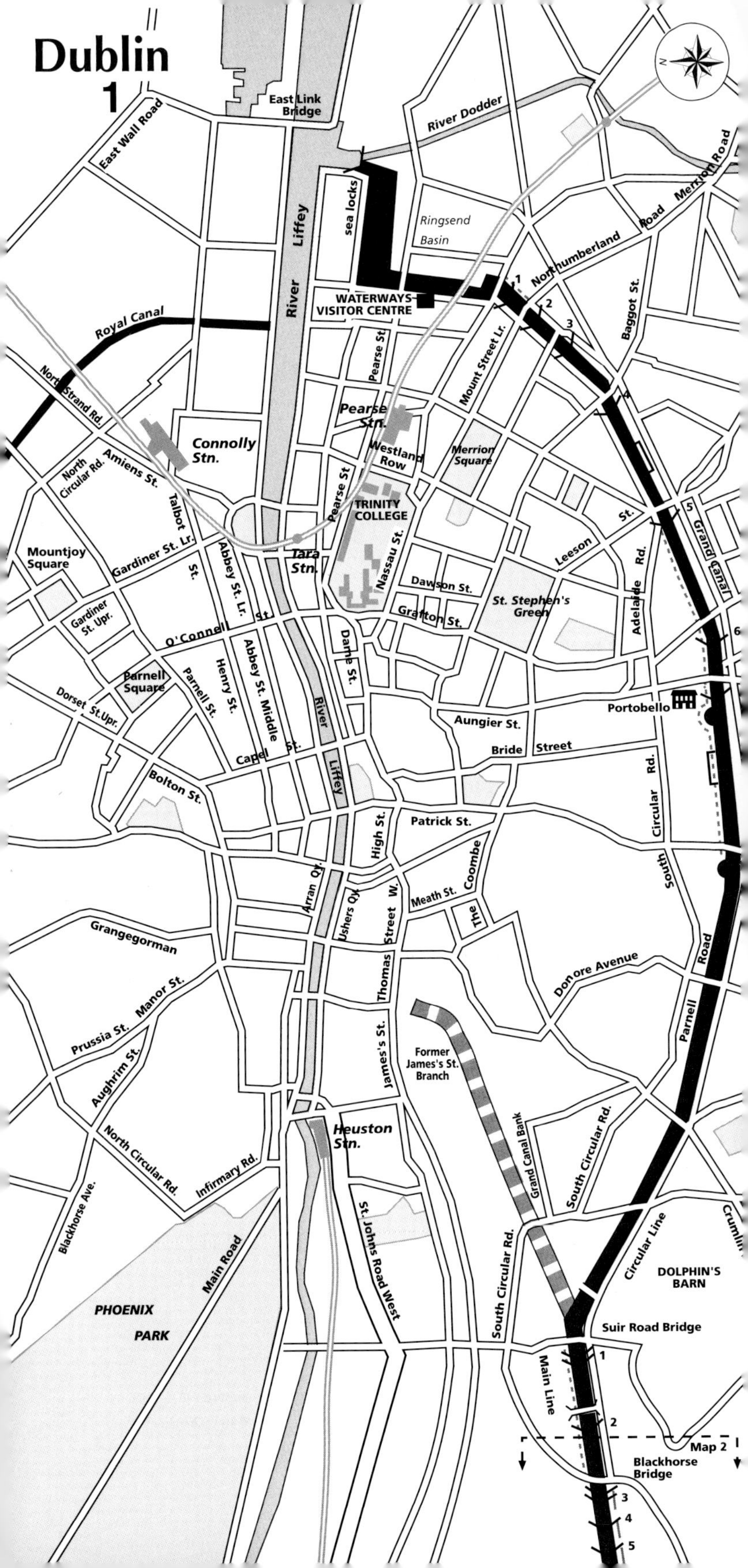

Dublin
1
East Link Bridge
East Wall Road
River Dodder
Merrion Road
sea locks
River Liffey
Ringsend Basin
Northumberland Road
Baggot St.
WATERWAYS VISITOR CENTRE
Royal Canal
North Strand Rd.
Pearse St
Mount Street Lr.
Pearse Stn.
Connolly Stn.
Westland Row
Merrion Square
North Circular Rd.
Amiens St.
Talbot St.
Pearse St
TRINITY COLLEGE
Grand Canal
Leeson St.
Mountjoy Square
Gardiner St. Lr.
Abbey St. Lr.
Tara Stn.
Nassau St.
Dawson St.
Adelaide Rd.
Gardiner St. Upr.
O'Connell St.
Grafton St.
St. Stephen's Green
Dame St.
Parnell Square
Parnell St.
Henry St.
Abbey St. Middle
Dorset St.Upr.
River Liffey
Portobello
Aungier St.
Capel St.
Bride Street
Bolton St.
Circular Rd.
Patrick St.
High St.
South Road
Arran Qy.
Ushers Qy.
Meath St.
Coombe
The
Thomas Street W.
Grangegorman
Donore Avenue
Manor St.
Prussia St.
Aughrim St.
James's St.
Former James's St. Branch
Parnell
Heuston Stn.
North Circular Rd.
Infirmary Rd.
Grand Canal Bank
South Circular Rd.
Crumlin
Blackhorse Ave.
St. Johns Road West
Main Road
Circular Line
DOLPHIN'S BARN
PHOENIX PARK
South Circular Rd.
Suir Road Bridge
Main Line
Map 2
Blackhorse Bridge
1
2
3
4
5
6
1
2
3
4
5

Circular Line to Inchicore

1

Entrance to the Grand Canal system is through one of the sea locks from the tidal River Liffey, near the mouth of the River Dodder. For 2 hours either side of low water there is less than 3ft (0.9m) over the cill, but boats may tie up to the quay below the lock to wait for the tide.

Headroom under the bridge that separates the outer from the inner **Ringsend Basin** is about 8 ft 3 in (2.48m) at normal water level, but this bridge can be lifted. The exit from the inner basin is under an arched railway bridge with about 8ft 10in (2.65m) headroom in the centre. Owing to the curve of the arch there is less room in practice - 8ft 2in (2.45m) over a width of 10ft (3m). It is important to keep about 18 in (0.45m) from the camshire on the west bank to maximise headroom. There is a very difficult corner to negotiate before passing under **Maquay Bridge**. From here there are 7 locks close together and then a 2-mile (3 km) level from **Portobello** to **1st lock, Main Line,** which is at the junction of the **Circular Line** and the old line to **James's Street Harbour**, now filled in.

The road accompanies the canal all the way to **Blackhorse Bridge, Inchicore. 1st lock** is double-chambered but doubles count as one in the numbering system. Despite much time-consuming work by ***Dúchas* The Heritage Service** removing debris from the canal, some rubbish may be picked up by propellers, especially on deep-draught vessels. The best area for shopping and fuel is at **Baggot Street** (4th lock), but it is unfortunately not wise to leave a boat unattended in the city. There is a jetty above the 4th lock, convenient for Baggot Street, and another above the 7th lock at Portobello.

History Dublin's original canal terminus was **James's Street Harbour** beside the city basin, because one of the objectives of the canal builders was to provide a reliable source of drinking water. In 1790, with the canal completed to Athy, work began on the link with the Liffey. The more obvious route from James's Street was supplanted by an ambitious scheme following the recently completed Circular Road. With financial assistance from the Government the **Circular Line** and **Ringsend Docks** were completed and a lavish opening ceremony held on 23 April 1796. **Portobello Hotel** was opened in 1807 and became the passage boat terminus. It ceased to operate as an hotel in the 1850s and for many years was a hospital before being converted into offices. It is now an educational centre.

Locks Ringsend sea locks — George Brierly, The Dockhouse, Ringsend. Tel: (01) 668 9466

Circular Line

No.	Lock	Rise	Contact
1	Maquay Br.	3.0 ft rise	
2	Lr. Mount St.	8.7 ft rise	
3	Up. Mount St.	9.9 ft rise	
4	Baggot St.	8.2 ft rise	
5	Leeson St.	7.9 ft rise	Stephen Brierly
6	Charlemont St.	10.9 ft rise	Tel: (01) 660 1710
7	Portobello	8.3 ft rise	

Main Line

No.	Lock	Rise	Contact
1	(double)	14.4 ft rise	
2		12.8 ft rise	Ray Moore
3	(double)	19.1 ft rise	Tel: (086) 827 8025
4		13.0 ft rise	

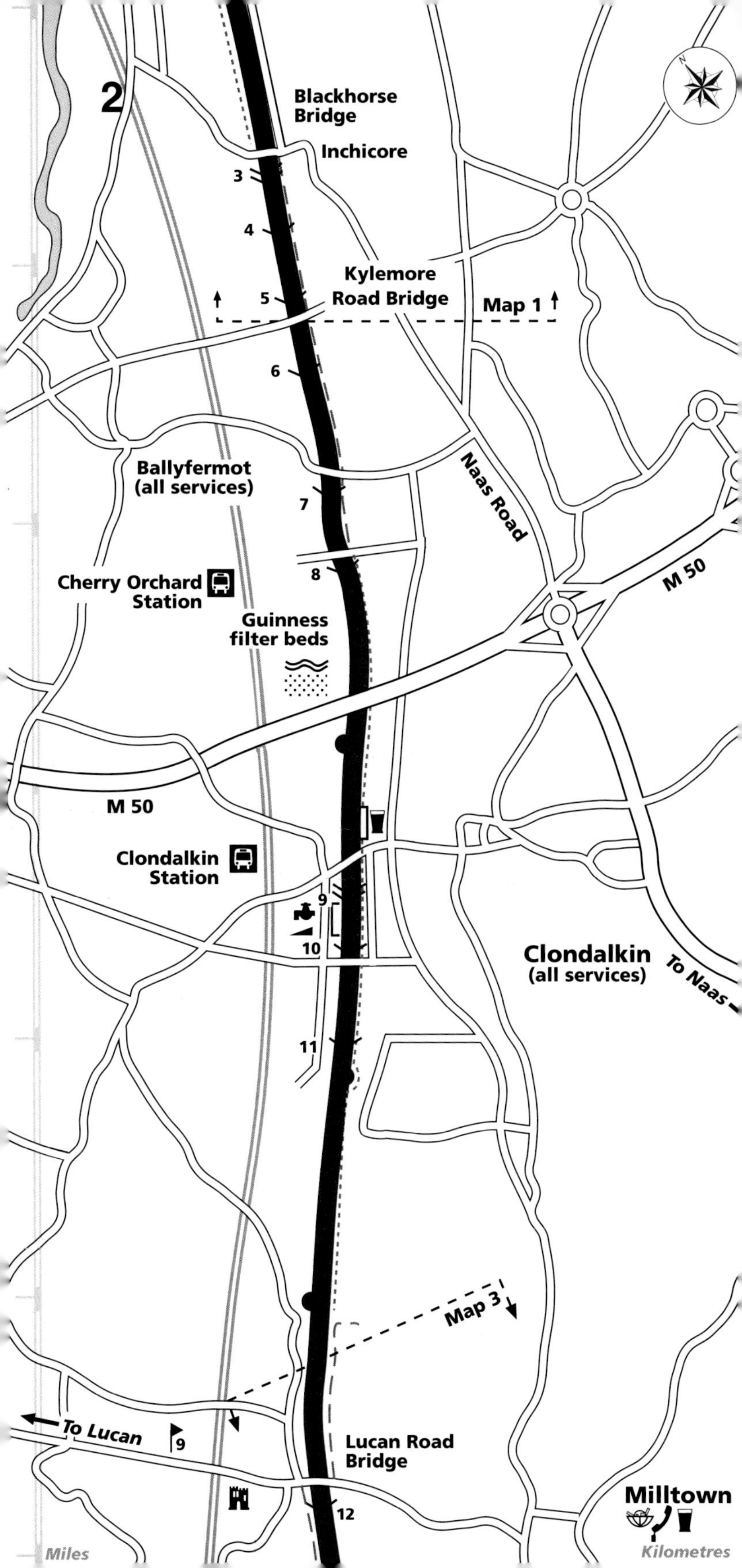
2
Blackhorse
Bridge
Inchicore
3
4
Kylemore
Road Bridge
5
Map 1
6
Ballyfermot
(all services)
Naas Road
7
Cherry Orchard
Station
8
M 50
Guinness
filter beds
M 50
Clondalkin
Station
9
10
Clondalkin
(all services)
To Naas
11
Map 3
To Lucan
9
Lucan Road
Bridge
12
Milltown
Miles
Kilometres

Blackhorse Bridge, Inchicore to 12th Lock, Lucan Road Bridge **2**

The canal rises steeply out of the city, but this is an unattractive area and it is the stretch of canal most subject to vandalism. It is wise to make a point of taking locks 1 to 9 early in the morning, or during school hours, to avoid the sometimes boisterous attentions of children. Despite much time-consuming work by ***Dúchas*** **The Heritage Service** removing debris from the canal, some rubbish may be picked up by propellers, especially on deep-draught vessels.

Above **8th lock** are the filter beds from which Messrs Guinness used to draw the soft water that was so suitable for brewing. The filter beds are still in use today, but the water is used for washing purposes only.

There is a jetty below the **9th lock**, and a slip and a quay wall above the lock. **Clondalkin** is an area of rapid industrial growth and a new town has sprung up with well-stocked shops. Housing estates turned their backs on the canal, unaware of its amenity value. However in recent years local community groups have carried out works to enhance the canal environment and to improve the towpath for walkers.

Above **11th lock** the canal at last emerges into a country setting.

History Just below **8th lock** a passage boat filled and sank one Christmas evening in 1792 with the loss of 11 lives; the accident was said to have been caused by the riotous behaviour of the passengers. Clondalkin has a fine round tower, a large stone cross and the remains of an early monastery.

11th lock was the first lock to be built by Thomas Omer in 1756; he started here because it was more difficult and expensive to buy land near the city. Omer envisaged a canal on a larger scale, and his three locks (11 to 13) were subsequently shortened by half and the width reduced by narrowing each end. The remains of the original tail-gate recesses are still visible below **11th** and **12th lock.** A small two-storied house above **11th lock** is typical of Omer's lock-houses. **Lucan Road Bridge** crosses the lower half of Omer's lock and a short distance above **12th lock** there is another of his lock-houses, occupied and in good repair. There were formerly many mills between here and the city but Grange Mills is the only one to have survived. Adamstown Castle, a sixteenth-century tower house, lies to the north of **12th lock** between the canal and the railway.

Locks			
	5	10.1 ft rise	Ray Moore
	6	10.9 ft rise	Tel: (086) 827 8025
	7	12.3 ft rise	
	8	8.3 ft rise	Donal O'Brien lives
	9 (double)	15.0 ft rise	at 9th lock
	10	10.1 ft rise	Tel: (01) 459 3598
	11	10.5 ft rise	
	12	12.4 ft rise	Ray Moore
			Tel: (086) 827 8025

Facilities **Pubs:** Ballyfermot Bridge; Clondalkin Bridge; Milltown.
All Services: Clondalkin; Ballyfermot.
Slip: 9th Lock, Clondalkin.

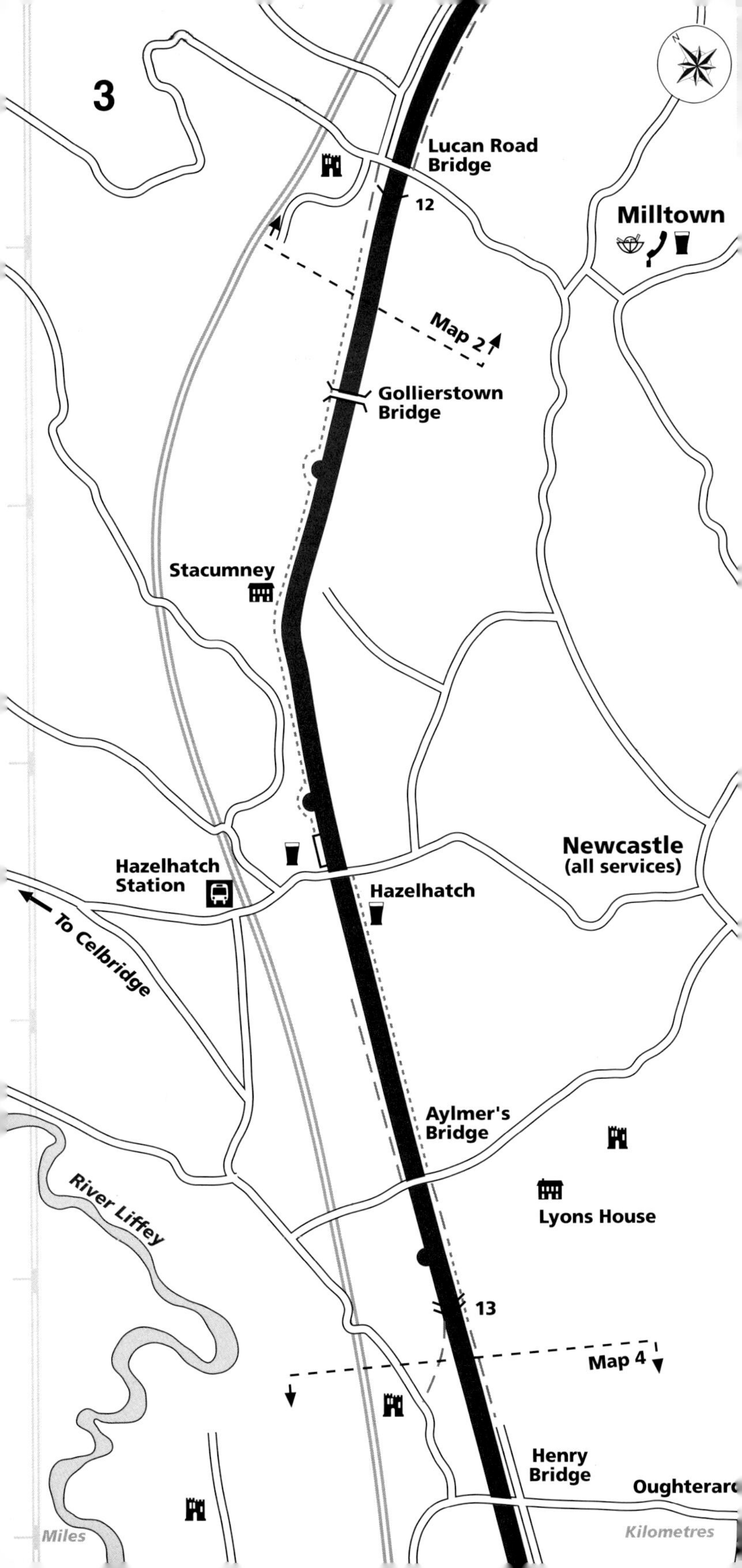

3
Lucan Road
Bridge
12
Milltown
Map 2
Gollierstown
Bridge
Stacumney
Hazelhatch
Station
To Celbridge
Hazelhatch
Newcastle
(all services)
Aylmer's
Bridge
River Liffey
Lyons House
13
Map 4
Henry
Bridge
Oughterard
Miles
Kilometres

Lucan Road Bridge to Henry Bridge, Ardclough 3

From **12th lock** the canal gradually enters a cutting as it approaches **Gollierstown Bridge**. Having emerged from the cutting at Stacumney the canal is carried on an embankment towards **Hazelhatch Bridge.** There are fine views from the embankment of the Dublin mountains away to the south.

Passing under **Aylmer's Bridge,** the canal skirts Lyons demesne with its many fine trees. Part of the estate is now an agricultural college for University College Dublin, and part is being developed as a leisure centre.

History Omer deliberately routed his canal through the limestone quarries at **Gollierstown**, as this made it easier to transport the stone which was to be used for building locks and bridges along the line. By doing so, however, he added greatly to the difficulties of constructing the canal itself. John Smeaton, who visited Ireland in 1773 at the request of the newly-formed Grand Canal Company, criticised him for this decision.

Omer, like many other early canal engineers, did not follow contours, hence the cuttings and embankments which are a feature of this stretch of canal.

There was a store-yard and another of Omer's lock-houses at **Stacumney**. Known locally as "the hulk", it was at one time leased to people visiting nearby Lucan spa to partake of the waters. **Hazelhatch Bridge** was originally made of wood but it was replaced by this handsome stone bridge when it was reported that passengers were in danger if they did not duck smartly. **Newcastle** was a garrison town for the Norman "Pale" and has an interesting early church tower, old glebe house and castle. **Lyons House** was formerly the home of the Cloncurrys. The 2nd Lord Cloncurry, who died in 1853, played an active part in the political and economic growth of the country, and was one of the early directors of the canal company. There are a number of interesting castles in the area, constructed to protect the "Pale", one being in the Lyons estate.

In order to correct an error in the levels an extra lock had to be built between Hazelhatch and Aylmer's Bridge. In 1783 this extra lock was removed and **13th lock,** the next one down the line, was converted into a double lock. The large lower gate recesses and the strange shape of the upper chamber are remnants of Omer's original larger lock. There was once a large mill above the lock, but this was destroyed by fire. **Aylmer's** and **Henry Bridges** record the names of local landlords who possibly financed the building or assisted the company in the purchase of land for the canal.

Locks 13 (double) 16.1 ft rise Ray Moore
Tel: (086) 827 8025

Facilities **Pubs:** Hazelhatch.
All Services: Newcastle, 2 miles (3 km) south from Hazelhatch Bridge.

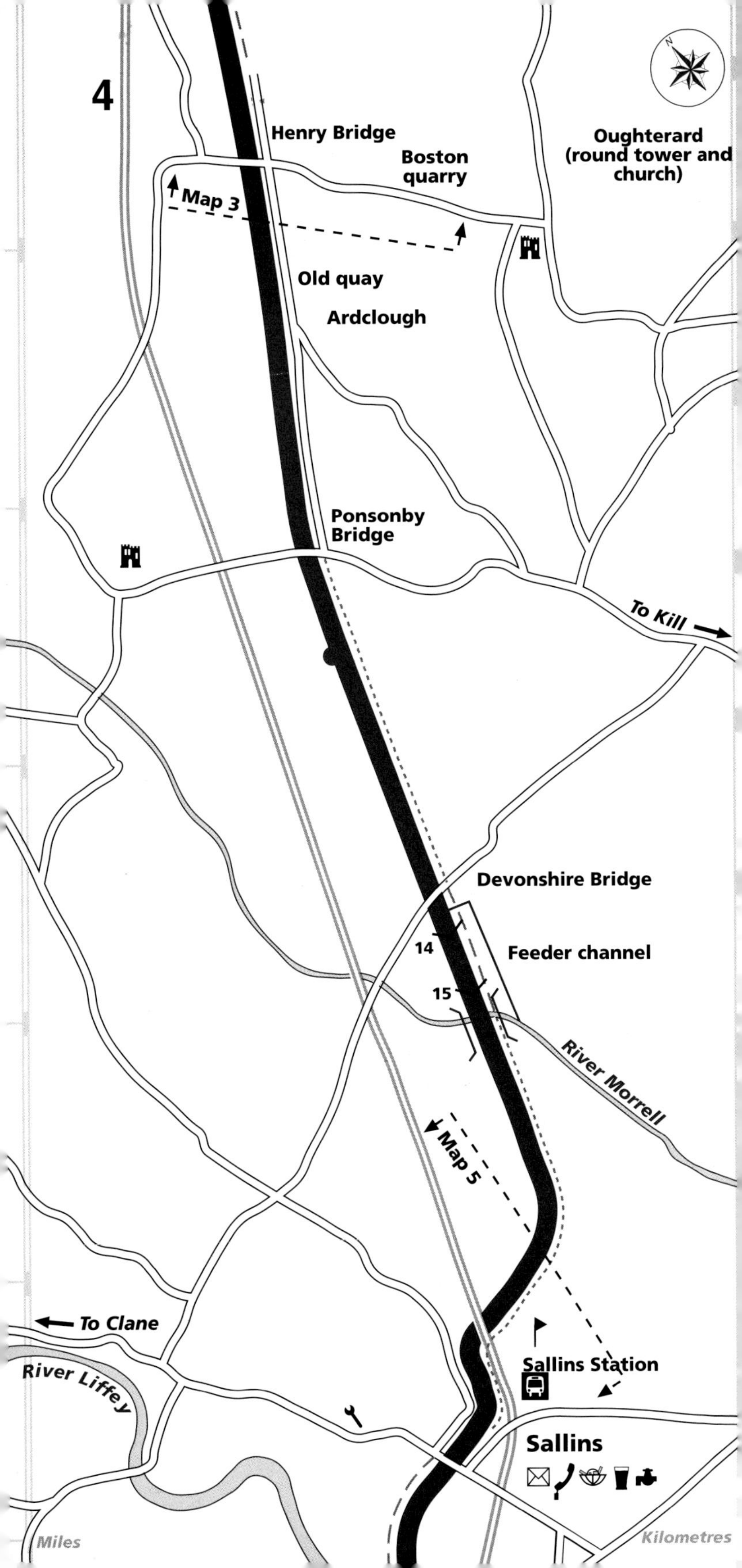
4
Henry Bridge
Boston quarry
Oughterard (round tower and church)
Map 3
Old quay
Ardclough
Ponsonby Bridge
To Kill
Devonshire Bridge
14
Feeder channel
15
River Morrell
Map 5
To Clane
Sallins Station
River Liffey
Sallins
Miles
Kilometres

Henry Bridge to Sallins

4

Ponsonby Bridge was known to old canal men as "the eleven mile bridge", probably 11 Irish miles (which are 2,240 yards) from James's Street Harbour. The next stretch of canal is again embanked.

The Morrell Feeder enters from the south beyond **Devonshire Bridge** and care should be taken to allow for the current. The feeder is a short artificial cut which is taken from the River Morrell, a tributary of the Liffey, and controlled by a sluice near the old lock-house beside **15th lock.**

Above **15th lock** the canal crosses the Morrell by a small aqueduct. A secluded and well-wooded stretch of canal follows and, passing under the main railway line from Dublin to Cork, the canal enters **Sallins.** The narrow road bridge over the canal was sensitively widened by Kildare County Council in 1988.

History

At **Oughterard** there is an interesting ruined church and round tower. Arthur Guinness, founder of Guinness's Brewery in 1759, who "departed this life on 23rd January, 1803" is buried here. **Ardclough** was once a busy hamlet serving the nearby Boston Quarry but the overgrown quay is now scarcely discernible.

It was the anticipation of obtaining water from the Morrell for the thirsty citizens of Dublin which prompted Dublin Corporation to take an active part in the construction of the canal in the early years. The supply began in 1777 and continued to be the principal source of drinking water until the Vartry scheme came into operation in 1869.

The canal company fought the construction of railways and raised all sorts of objections about the railway bridge but the railways expanded and all passenger traffic ceased on the canal in 1852.

Near **Sallins,** on the north bank, is what is reputed to be the first mass concrete building erected in Ireland, built by a French company as a sugar processing plant. Close to the bridge at **Sallins** was an old canal hotel, now demolished. Built in the 1780s by the canal company, it was too near Dublin and was never a commercial success. It was at the bridge at **Sallins** on 21st January 1777 that the directors of the canal company arrived in 10 post-chaises to receive the resignation of John Trail, their engineer, who had failed to carry out his contract to complete the canal to the Liffey.

Locks	14	7.1 ft rise	Martin Fogarty
	15	8.6 ft rise	based at 15th lock
			Tel: (045) 896 300

Facilities **Shops, Pubs, Post-office:** Sallins.

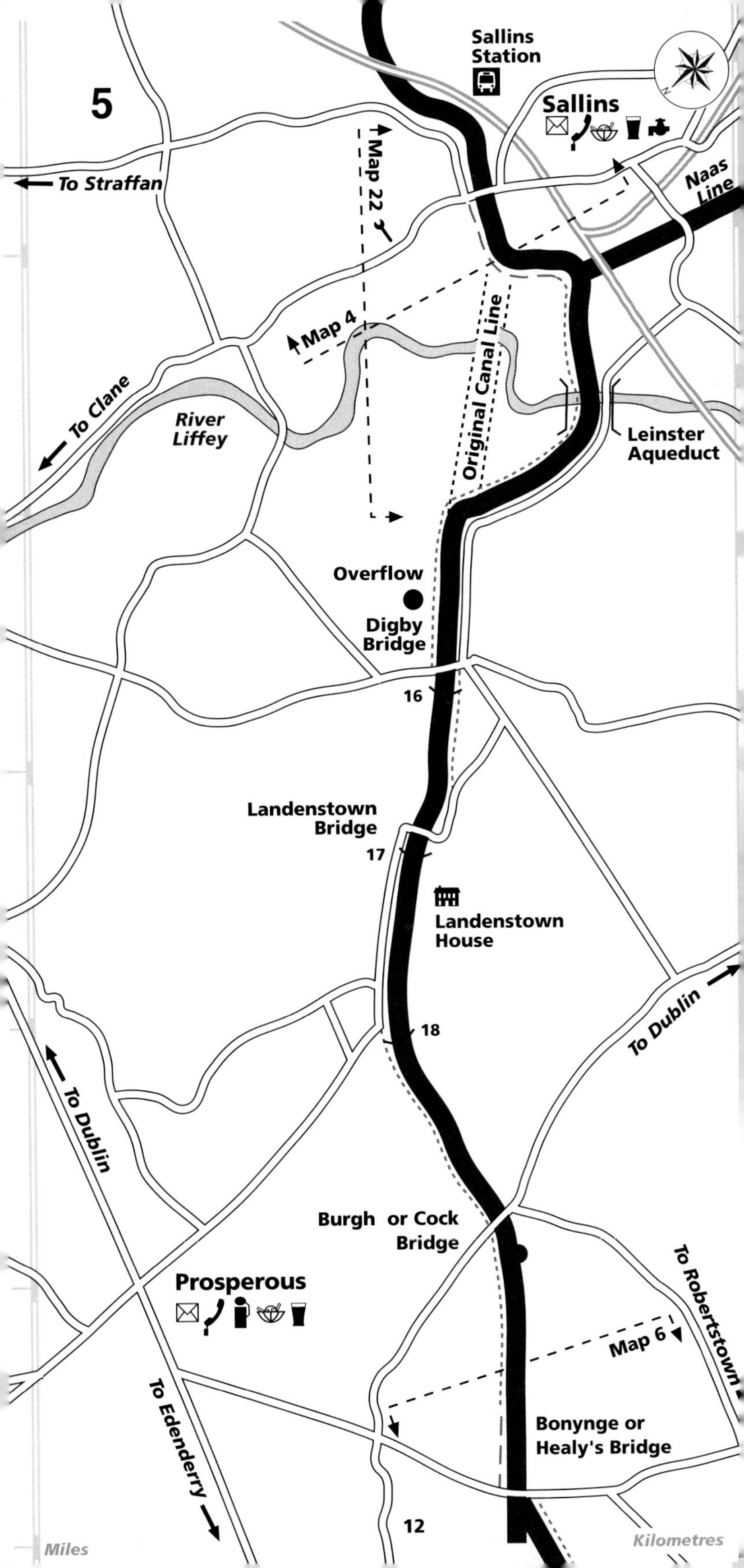
5
Sallins Station
Sallins
To Straffan
Map 22
Naas Line
Map 4
To Clane
River Liffey
Original Canal Line
Leinster Aqueduct
Overflow
Digby Bridge
16
Landenstown Bridge
17
Landenstown House
18
To Dublin
To Dublin
Burgh or Cock Bridge
Prosperous
To Robertstown
Map 6
To Edenderry
Bonynge or Healy's Bridge
12
Miles
Kilometres

Sallins to Bonynge or Healy's Bridge **5**

Not far from Sallins the canal makes a double bend in preparation for the Liffey crossing, passing an old dry dock and Soldier's Island, the entrance to the **Naas Branch** (Maps 22 and 23). The **Leinster Aqueduct** is a fine structure and a short walk upstream reveals a good view of it. A footpath under the aqueduct links the towpaths on the north and south banks of the canal. The Liffey is a confusing river: it rises only 15 miles (24 km) from Dublin but curves around taking 92 miles (147 km) to reach the sea, and at this point it is flowing north.

Between the aqueduct and **Digby Bridge** there is an overflow on the north bank. Built in four circular basins to prevent erosion, it was known to the canal men as "the big pot, the little pot, the boolawn and the skillet".

At **17th lock** are the entrance gates to **Landenstown House** and the canal skirts the demesne lined by magnificent beeches. This is the headquarters of the Prosperous Angling Club and there is good coarse fishing but "Prosperous" is a place name not an adjective. The village lies 2 miles (3 km) to the north.

18th lock is the last rising lock and a summit level of 5.5 miles (9 km) lies ahead. The towpath between **18th lock** and **Cock Bridge** can be very wet and muddy in winter. The canal gradually narrows as it nears **Cock Bridge** and enters a cutting with overhanging trees. The canal has been passing around the Hill of Downings which contains a particularly good type of clay for lining the canal. Beyond **Cock Bridge** there are signs of extensive clay workings.

History Omer originally intended to cross the Liffey downstream and a walk from the first bend after **Sallins** towards the river will reveal signs of his excavations and preparations for a lock.

The **Naas Branch** was completed to the town of Naas in 1789 by another company but it ran into financial difficulties and was taken over by the Grand Canal Company.

The **Leinster Aqueduct** was built by Richard Evans who later joined the Royal Canal Company and was the engineer of much of its early works.

Shortly after the canal was opened, side chambers were built at **16th** and **17th locks** to conserve water as the supply from the Morrell proved to be insufficient. Much later the Grand Canal Company built a pumping station at the **Leinster Aqueduct** to raise water from the Liffey to the canal. This was taken over shortly afterwards (1947) by the Electricity Supply Board when it agreed to accept the responsibility for maintaining a navigable depth of water in return for extracting water from the canal for the cooling tower of the power station at Allenwood. The pumps were taken over by ***Dúchas* The Heritage Service** after the closure of the power station.

Landenstown House was built for the Digby family about 1740; Simon Digby MP was one of the early directors of the company.

Locks	16	8.9 ft rise	Martin Fogarty
	17	8.0 ft rise	based at 15th lock
	18	5.1 ft rise	Tel: (045) 896 300
			(summit level 279.1 ft OD)

Facilities **Shops, Garage, Pubs, Post-office:** Prosperous, about 2 miles (3 km) north of 18th lock.

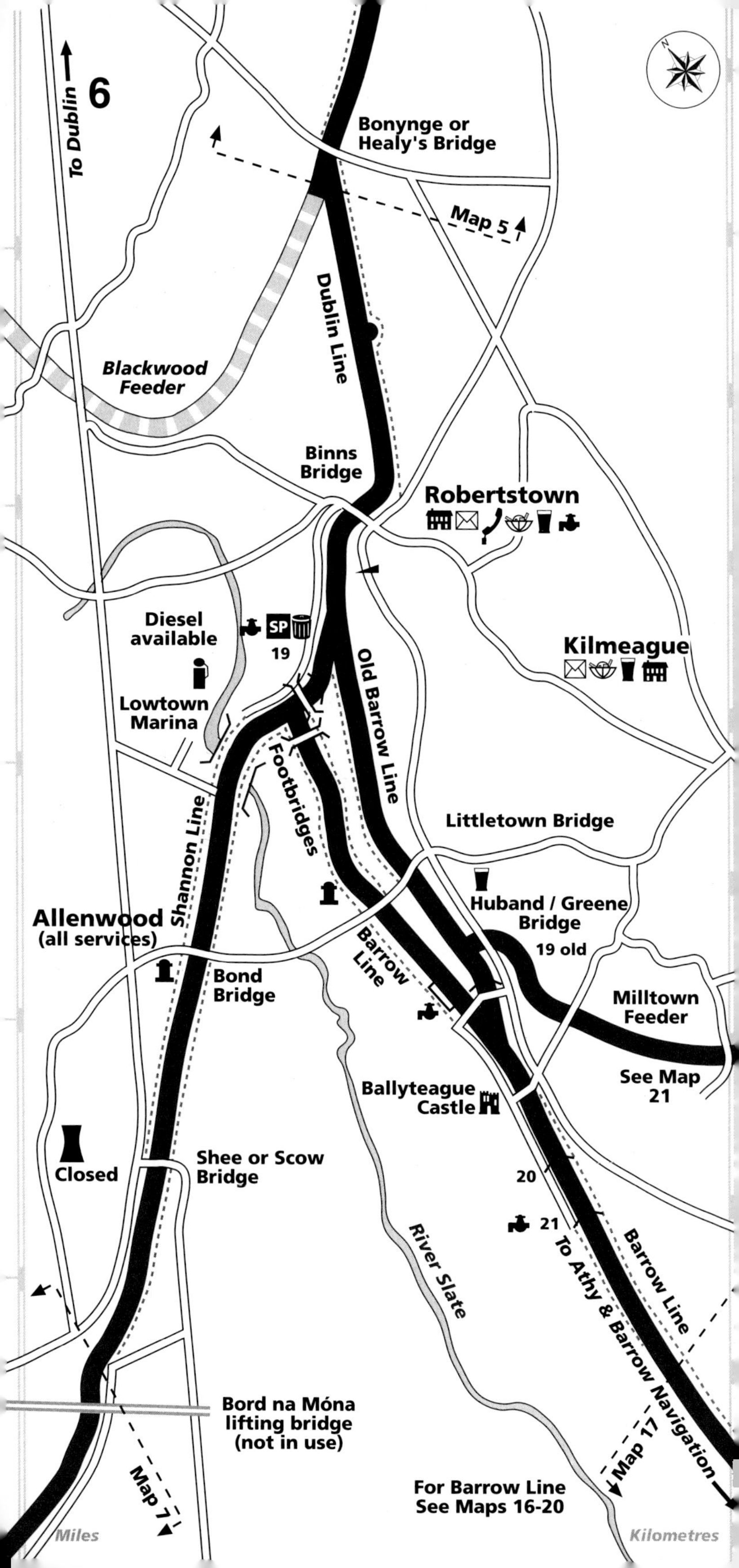
6
To Dublin
Bonynge or
Healy's Bridge
Map 5
Dublin Line
Blackwood
Feeder
Binns
Bridge
Robertstown
Diesel
available
SP
19
Kilmeague
Lowtown
Marina
Old Barrow Line
Footbridges
Shannon Line
Littletown Bridge
Allenwood
(all services)
Huband / Greene
Bridge
19 old
Barrow
Line
Bond
Bridge
Milltown
Feeder
See Map
21
Ballyteague
Castle
Closed
Shee or Scow
Bridge
20
21
River Slate
To Athy & Barrow Navigation
Barrow Line
Bord na Móna
lifting bridge
(not in use)
Map 7
Map 17
For Barrow Line
See Maps 16-20
Miles
Kilometres

Bonynge or Healy's Bridge to Bord na Móna Railway Bridge

At **Healy's Bridge** the Blackwood water supply used to enter the canal; 4 miles (6.5 km) long, it was a controlled supply, fed by an artificial reservoir. The canal is carried on an embankment through the Bog of Moods to **Robertstown.**

Above **19th lock**, the end of the summit level, the old Barrow Line carrying water from the Milltown supply joins the Main Line. The feeder is navigable to **Milltown Bridge** (about 6 miles (10 km)) for very shallow draught boats, but is obstructed by a low bridge (about 6 ft 6 in (1.95m)) near **Kilmeague**. It continues on to springs near Pollardstown, whose crystal clear waters are the canal's principal supply (Map 21).

Below **19th lock** the old coal stores have been converted into Lowtown Marina, a boat yard and hire-boat base where diesel is available. The new Barrow Line branches off to the south and the Main Line continues on over 2 small aqueducts, the first of these over the Slate which is good for trout fishing.

The local community in Allenwood has developed an interesting series of linked walking routes using the canal towpath, forest tracks and paths across the bogs.

History

The **Blackwood Feeder** was closed in 1952 and sold off. It is now partly filled in. The early engineers did not allow for subsidence in crossing the Bog of Moods, a mistake they repeated at the bog west of Ticknevin. Subsidence of up to 16ft (4.9m.) occurred and in the end the canal had to be carried on a high embankment.

Robertstown Hotel was opened in 1801, and an extension was added in 1804. Business was good in the early days, but revenue began to fall in 1808. Gradually the 72 windows and 62 hearths were closed up to avoid paying tax. In 1849 it ceased to be a hotel. In 1869, after long negotiaions, the building was leased to the Royal Irish Constabulary, who used it as a barracks until 1905. In more recent years it has had a number of uses, and is being developed as a Community Centre at present. There are trips on converted canal boats in summer.

The coalyard was constructed in 1808 by the Grand Canal Company in conjunction with the leasing of the collieries near Castle comer in an attempt to increase trade.

Shee Bridge is known locally as "Scow Bridge", probably a corruption of "skew"; it is the only oblique-arched bridge on the canal, apart from the later railway arch at Ringsend.

Locks			
	19 (Lowtown)	7.9 ft fall	James Conroy Tel: (045) 860 237
	19 (Old Barrow Line)	7.9 ft fall	Peter Goulding

Facilities

All Services: Allenwood.
Shops, Pubs, Post-office: Robertstown; Kilmeague (about 2 miles (3 km) from Robertstown).
Slip: Robertstown, west of Binn's Bridge.
Water, Rubbish Disposal, Pump-out Station: Lock 19, Main Line.

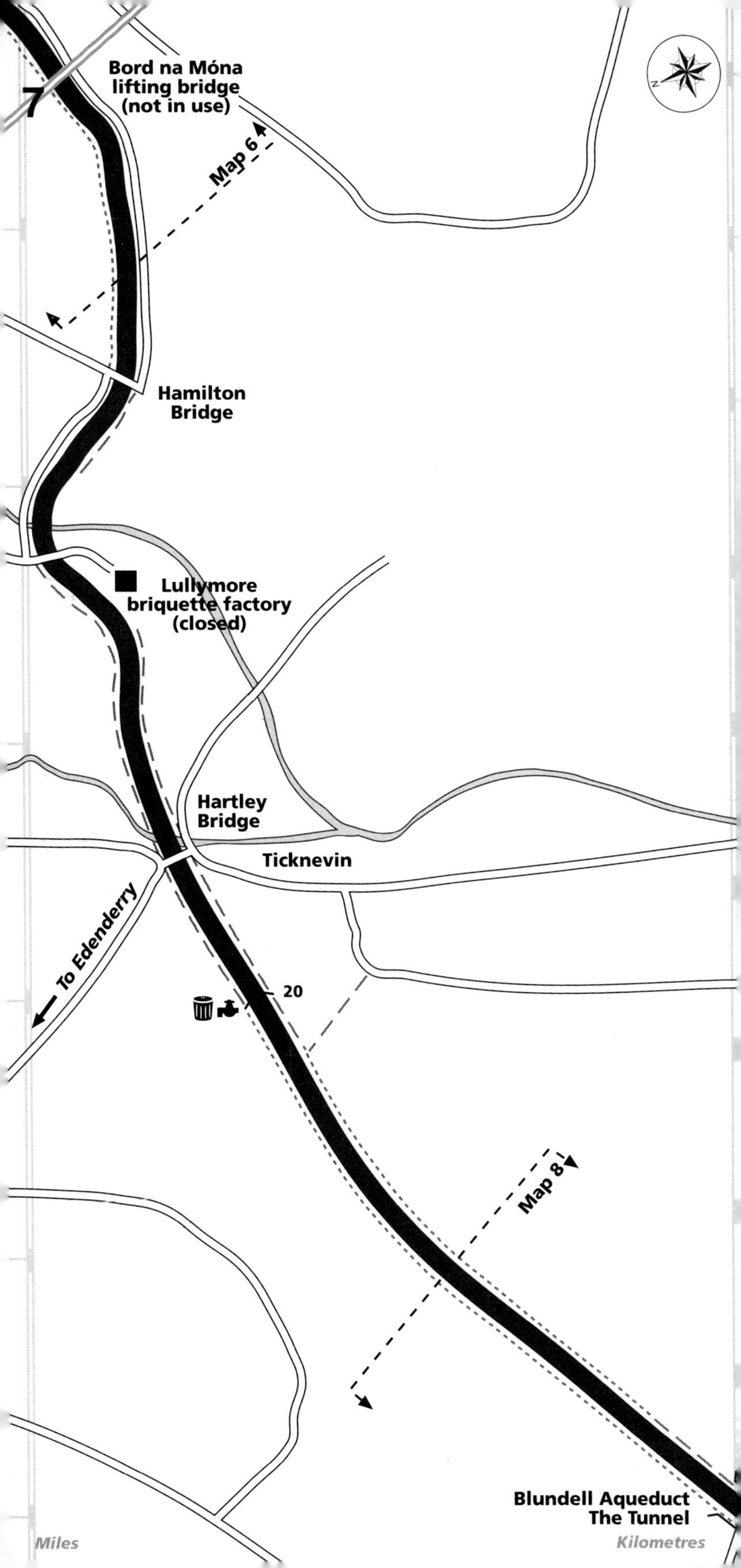

7
Bord na Móna
lifting bridge
(not in use)
Map 6
Hamilton
Bridge
Lullymore
briquette factory
(closed)
Hartley
Bridge
Ticknevin
To Edenderry
20
Map 8
Blundell Aqueduct
The Tunnel
Miles
Kilometres

Bord na Móna Railway Bridge to Blundell Aqueduct **7**

The stretch to **Hamilton Bridge** is very popular with local and visiting fishermen. It is interesting to compare the style of the 1796 **Hamilton Bridge** with the 1949 **Kilpatrick Bridge.**

This is a pretty section especially when the hawthorn is in bloom. **20th** lock ends this 7-mile (11 km) level and the canal stretches away into the distance across the bog without another lock for 18.5 miles (30 km). The canal skirts the northern limit of the bog with poor scrub to the north. **Blundell Aqueduct**, known locally as "the Tunnel", carries the canal across the Edenderry-Rathangan road.

History

There have been many efforts over the years to exploit the bogs. In the 1850s the Irish Amelioration Society set up works near **Allenwood** to make charcoal out of turf, without much success. The briquette factory was erected in 1934, but ran into financial and technical trouble and was taken over by the Turf Development Board, the forerunner of Bord na Móna. It was closed in 1993.

20th lock used to have side-chambers and the hole in the wall of the chamber is visible, but the ponds have been filled in.

One tends to think of aqueducts and tunnels as the most impressive and difficult canal works, but this stretch of canal across the bog was one of the most difficult engineering feats ever attempted before or, indeed, since. It took nearly 10 years to complete and many times the engineers felt like abandoning it for another route. These engineers, including John Smeaton, did not anticipate the enormous subsidence. Smeaton advised that the canal should be run through the bog at the original level, time was not allowed for subsidence and, once again, the engineers were faced with the task of securing high embankments. Looking to the south one can see the land rising to the original level of the bog beyond the range of the drainage caused by the canal works. In order to construct the canal a series of drains were opened, crossed by transverse drains, and the material excavated was dried in the squares created by the drains and was then wheeled to the canal to form the embankments. The channel along the top of the embankment was then lined with clay to hold the water in. The traveller today could well spare a thought for the men who laboured through 10 winters to achieve this remarkable stretch of canal.

In recent years extensive reconstruction has been carried out to the bog embankments between **20th lock** and the **Blundell Aqueduct.** There is little trace to be seen above the water of these major engineering works which will maintain the stability of the embankments for future years.

Locks	20	8.7 ft fall	John Pender Tel: (0405) 53 117

Facilities **Water, Rubbish Disposal:** Lock 20.

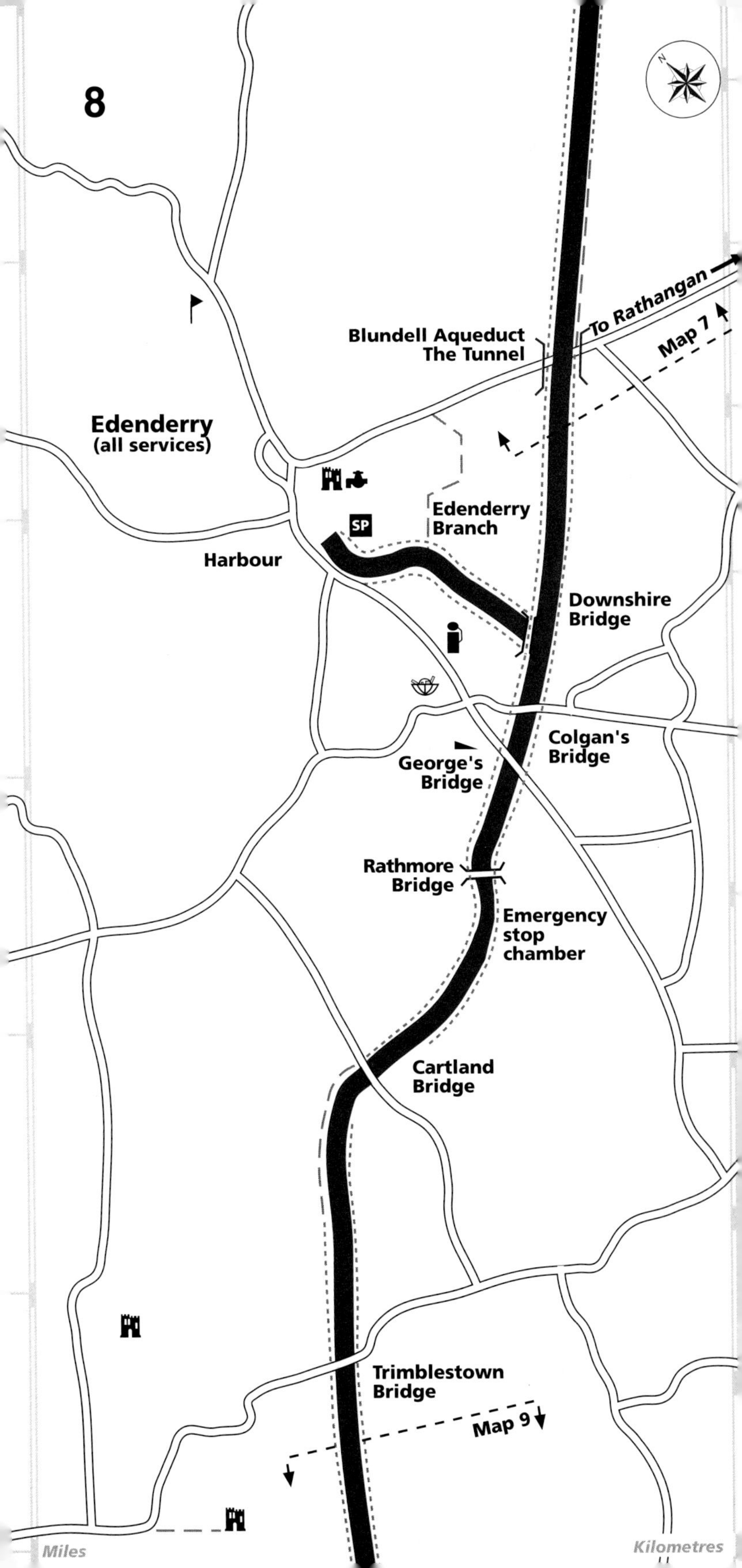
8
To Rathangan
Blundell Aqueduct
The Tunnel
Map 7
Edenderry
(all services)
Edenderry
Branch
SP
Harbour
Downshire
Bridge
Colgan's
Bridge
George's
Bridge
Rathmore
Bridge
Emergency
stop
chamber
Cartland
Bridge
Trimblestown
Bridge
Map 9
Miles
Kilometres

Blundell Aqueduct to Trimblestown Bridge **8**

Due to the shallow sloping sides of the canal between the Blundell Aqueduct and Downshire Bridge, boats should keep to the centre of the channel and away from the banks.

The canal continues, carried on a high embankment, to the entrance to the **Edenderry Branch**. This canal is 1 mile (1.5 km) long without any locks and winds its way up to an attractive harbour in the heart of the town. Approaching **Colgan's Bridge**, the crossing of the bog accomplished, the scenery returns to the familiar hedgerows.

Colgan's Bridge and **George's Bridge** are close together. The latter has been replaced by a modern structure which presents an ugly appearance to the canal and one feels that the engineers reluctantly allowed sufficient headroom for the boats.

For the next few miles the canal seems to detach itself from the busy world. **Rathmore Bridge** serves no road - it is an accommodation bridge, built to accommodate the farmer whose land was divided when the canal was cut. An emergency stop chamber has recently been constructed immediately west of Rathmore Bridge. Should a breach occur in the future, the stop-gates are designed to close automatically, limiting the loss of water from the canal and the damage to the embankments. **Ballybrittan Castle** is about 1 mile (1.5 km) to the north of **Trimblestown Bridge**.

History The embankment between the **Blundell Aqueduct** and the **Edenderry Branch** has caused a great deal of trouble over the years. A few hundred yards west of the aqueduct, on the north bank, major breaches occurred in 1797, shortly after the canal was opened, and in 1800, 1916 and 1989. The latest breach in 1989 was by far the most serious, and took about one year to repair at a cost of over £1 million. The embankment had to be rebuilt, and the channel relined using modern materials to prevent seepage. In an innovative measure aquatic reeds were transplanted along the water's edge of the repaired section. The plants help to prevent bank erosion by absorbing the wave energy caused by boats and wind, and they create an important habitat for fish, birds and aquatic invertebrates.

The Edenderry Branch, financed by the local landlord, Lord Downshire, was built at the same time as the Main Line, but the harbour was not finally completed until 1802. On a hill near the harbour stands the ruins of Blundell Castle. Lord Downshire married into the Blundell family and he proved a good landlord carrying out many improvements in the town.

At **Drumcooley**, on the south bank, opposite the entrance to the **Edenderry Branch**, there was a peat litter factory until 1945. It was started by Norman Palmer who originally conveyed turf to a factory in an old mill at 2nd lock in Dublin but, when it was burnt down, he moved operations to **Drumcooley.**

Colgan was the name of the owner of the house at the bridge who kept a waiting room for passengers in the old days. On one occasion he was reprimanded for failing to keep it open when a young lady passenger found herself deposited "at 11 o'clock of a dark night without any certainty of protection".

Facilities **All Services:** Edenderry.
Shop: at crossroads just north of Colgan's or George's Bridge.
Slip: George's Bridge, Edenderry.
Garage: on Edenderry Road.
Pump-out Station: Edenderry.

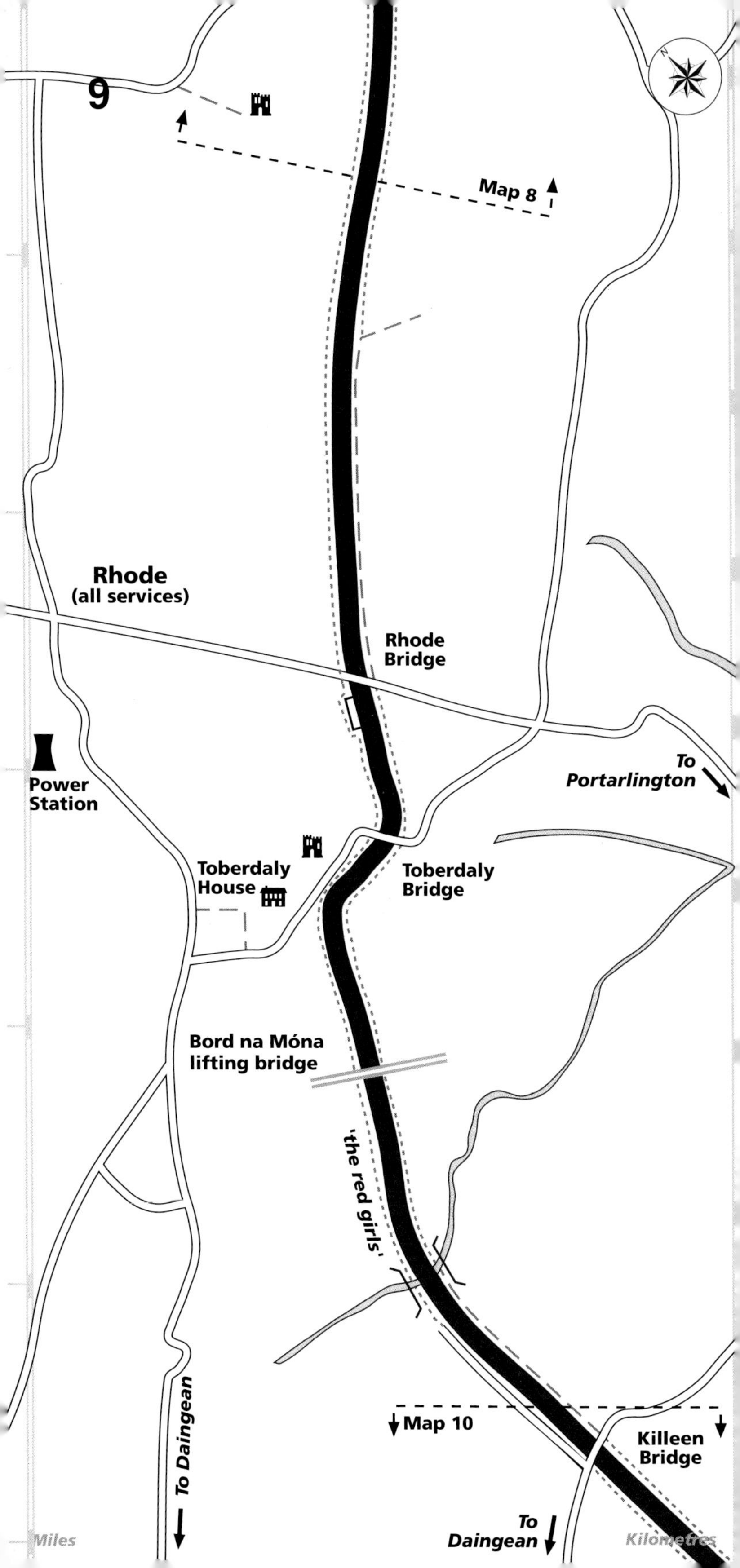

9
Map 8
Rhode
(all services)
Rhode
Bridge
To
Portarlington
Power
Station
Toberdaly
House
Toberdaly
Bridge
Bord na Móna
lifting bridge
'the red girls'
Map 10
Killeen
Bridge
To Daingean
To
Daingean
Miles
Kilometres

Trimblestown Bridge to Killeen Bridge

9

This is a very attractive stretch of canal with some forestry planting on the south side. There is a quay west of **Rhode Bridge** and from here it is about 1 mile (1.5 km) to the village of **Rhode.** Approaching **Toberdaly Bridge** there are some attractive stone cottages on the south side which must have been part of Toberdaly estate, and the ruins of the castle may be seen on the hill to the north. The twin towers of another turf-burning power station are prominent features, as is also Croghan Hill which has a prehistoric cairn on the summit. The canal takes a surprisingly sharp bend into **Toberdaly Bridge.**

Soon the trees give way to scrub land and more bog lies ahead with another **light railway bridge.** This bridge is in frequent use and has to be raised for boats to pass. There are mooring facilities both sides of the bridge on the north bank. Bord na Móna have a man on duty at the bridge when it is in use and leave it open for boats at other times.

History

Toberdaly Castle is well worth a visit; there are some people living in the houses in the yard who will allow you to look around. Apart from the castle, there seems to be ruins of other buildings dating from different periods with walled enclosures sloping down to the canal.

Near **Killeen Bridge** there is a stretch known to the old canal men as "The Red Girls" because at one time a family of auburn-haired beauties lived in a house along the bank.

Turf used to be one of the principal commodities carried on the canal and, during the "emergency years" in the 1940s, over 200,000 tons were shipped to Dublin in specially built boats. Recent development of the bogs has made no use of the canal but has used a network of light railways. The modern system, which is also used in Russia, is to pulverise the turf, air dry it and then transport it to the nearby power station where it is blown into the furnaces at pressure.

An accident occurred one "severe, cold and wet night" in 1836 when a turf boat went aground near **Killeen Bridge** because the long level was lowered by an exceptionally strong west wind. The crew refused to lighten the load to move her and a passage boat was held up for 6 hours until a boat arrived from the opposite direction and they were able to transfer the passengers.

Facilities

All Services: Rhode, 1 mile (1.5 km) north of Rhode Bridge.

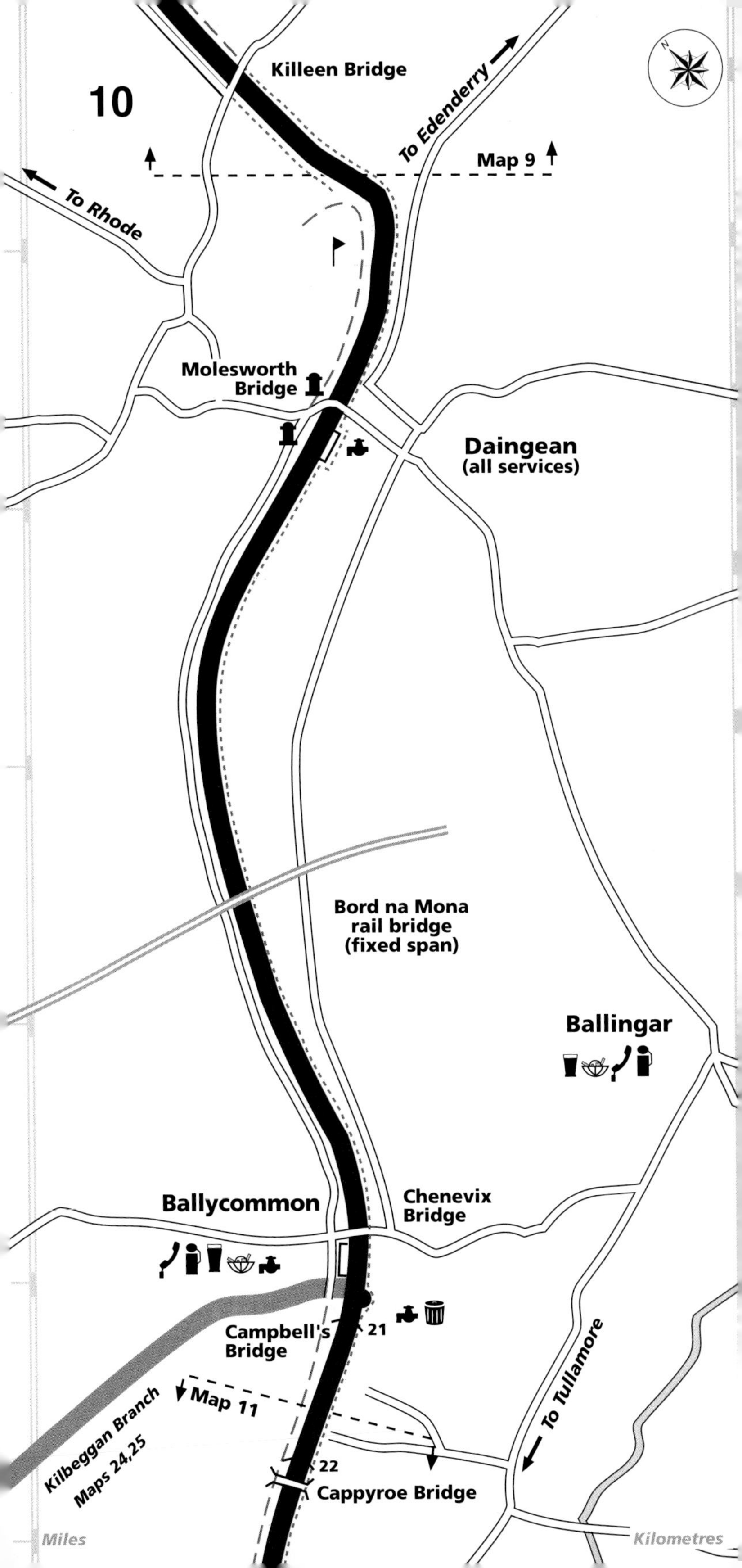

10
Killeen Bridge
To Edenderry
Map 9
To Rhode
Molesworth
Bridge
Daingean
(all services)
Bord na Mona
rail bridge
(fixed span)
Ballingar
Ballycommon
Chenevix
Bridge
Campbell's
Bridge
21
Map 11
To Tullamore
Kilbeggan Branch
Maps 24,25
22
Cappyroe Bridge
Miles
Kilometres

Killeen Bridge to Ballycommon

10

The canal converges with the main Edenderry-Tullamore road about 1 mile (1.5 km) from **Daingean**.There is a quay west of **Molesworth Bridge** in **Daingean.** On the opposite side of the canal are the forbidding walls of a former reformatory, now used as a store by the National Museum. The town is small, but the activity on the surrounding bogs has brought new prosperity to the area.

Leaving **Daingean** the canal passes through scrub land, poor agriculturally but rich in wildlife. Bord na Móna have rcently constructed a new fixed-span crossing for the light-rail system. The canal enters a short cutting and then the land falls away to the south as it approaches **Ballycommon**. There is a convenient quay to the west of the bridge, and mooring stakes on the north bank just east of the bridge.

A short distance below the bridge the **Kilbeggan Branch** (8 miles (13 km) long with no locks) used to join the Main Line but the entrance has now been sealed off and the bed is dry (Maps 24 and 25).

History

Daingean used to be the stronghold of the local chieftains, the O'Connors. In the 16th century, during the reign of Philip and Mary, the town was renamed Philipstown. It was once the assize town for the county, but this position was usurped in 1833 by the rapidly expanding town of Tullamore and thereafter Philipstown declined in importance. In 1920 the town reverted to its original name. The court house is attributed to James Gandon.

There used to be a sunken hull of an old flyboat here but it was removed some years ago. If, as the local people say, the flyboat was the *Hibernia* she was built in 1832 at Ringsend Iron Works by Courtney Clark. She was an imitation of the successful boats designed for the Paisley Canal by Houston but, although constructed of one-eighth-inch sheet iron, she proved too heavy to reach the critical speed of 7.5 mph required to make her rise on her own bow wave and eventually the canal company was forced to order hulls from Scotland.

Locks

21	8.8 ft fall	Overlapping Duties	James Fisher lives at 21st lock Tel: (0506) 53 084
22	8.7 ft fall		

Facilities

All Services: Daingean.
Shop, Garage, Pub, Telephone, Water: Ballycommon Bridge.
Water, Rubbish Disposal: Lock 21.

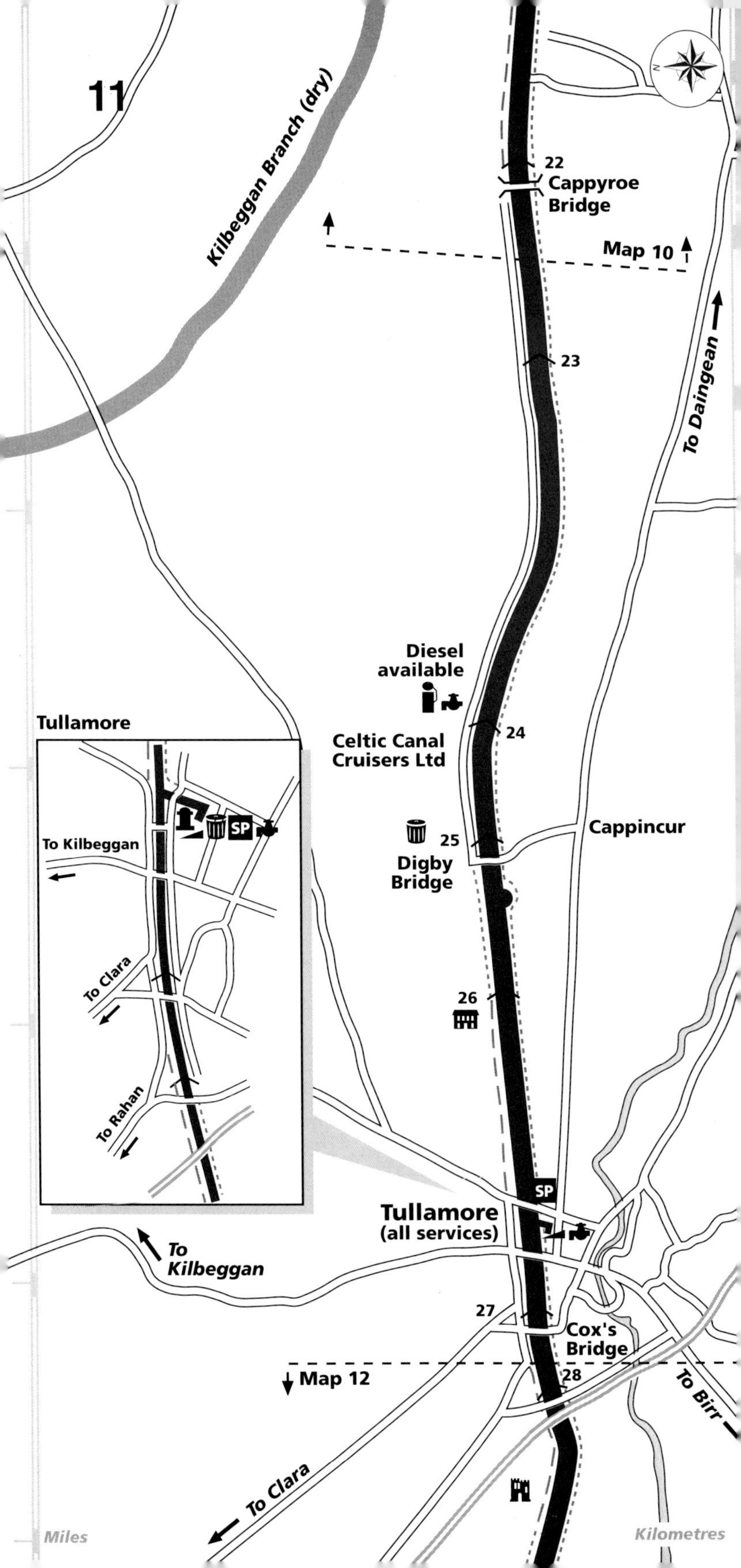
11
Kilbeggan Branch (dry)
22
Cappyroe Bridge
Map 10
23
To Daingean
Diesel available
24
Celtic Canal Cruisers Ltd
25
Cappincur
Digby Bridge
26
Tullamore
To Kilbeggan
SP
To Clara
To Rahan
SP
Tullamore (all services)
To Kilbeggan
27
Cox's Bridge
Map 12
28
To Birr
To Clara
Miles
Kilometres

Ballycommon to Tullamore

11

After travelling so many miles on the long level, the drop down into **Tullamore** seems to be very steep. At **24th lock** there is a hire-boat base, Celtic Canal Cruisers Ltd., where diesel and water are available.

The towpath between Cappincur and Tullamore is a pleasant walk, much used by the residents of the town.

The best moorings in **Tullamore** are up the short branch to the south to the old harbour. This is now the central engineering depot for the canal but suitable mooring has been provided for visiting boats outside the harbour. Like all large towns pilfering from boats can be a problem here. The shopping centre of the town lies to the south of the canal. The quay on the Main Line was formerly used by D.E. Williams, makers of the legendary Tullamore Dew and Irish Mist Whiskey.

History The lock-house at **26th lock**, known locally as "the Round Lock", was built by the contractor, Michael Hayes, on his own initiative and the directors refused to meet the "extra-ordinary and unnecessary" extra expense of £42.7.11d. Timber supports were put into this lock in 1812 because it was "bulging dangerously" and it was decided to postpone the permanent repair until a "more convenient season"!! The lock was repaired in 1993, and the timber supports finally removed. In 1999 the lock-house was restored, and is now open to the public at selected times.

Tullamore was the terminus of the canal for a number of years while the directors argued about how the line should be continued to the Shannon, and this is why they decided to build a harbour here. It originally contained a magnificent range of warehouses, but these were demolished in the 1940s.The attractive canal hotel on the branch was built in 1800-1 by the same contractor, Michael Hayes. It ceased to operate as a hotel in the 1830s and it was used as a presbytery from 1859 until 1974. Sadly it was the demolished to make way for a modern presbytery.

The Tullamore Dew Heritage Centre is located in the 1897 bonded warehouse on the canal bank at Bury Quay. The Centre explores the development of Tullamore, the arrival of the canal, the rise of the merchants and the role of the town's most famous product, Tullamore Dew Irish Whiskey. The Tourist Office is also in this building.

Locks

23	9.4 ft fall	Overlapping Duties	Cecil Murphy lives at 25th lock Tel: (0506) 41 686
24	9.8 ft fall		
25	9.5 ft fall		
26	9.6 ft fall		
27	8.1 ft fall		Leo Monaghan lives at 27th lock Tel: (0506) 51 363
28	8.7 ft fall		

Facilities **All Services:** Tullamore.
Slip, Water, Rubbish Disposal: Tullamore Harbour (office hours only).
Rubbish Disposal: Lock 25.
Pump-out Station: Tullamore.

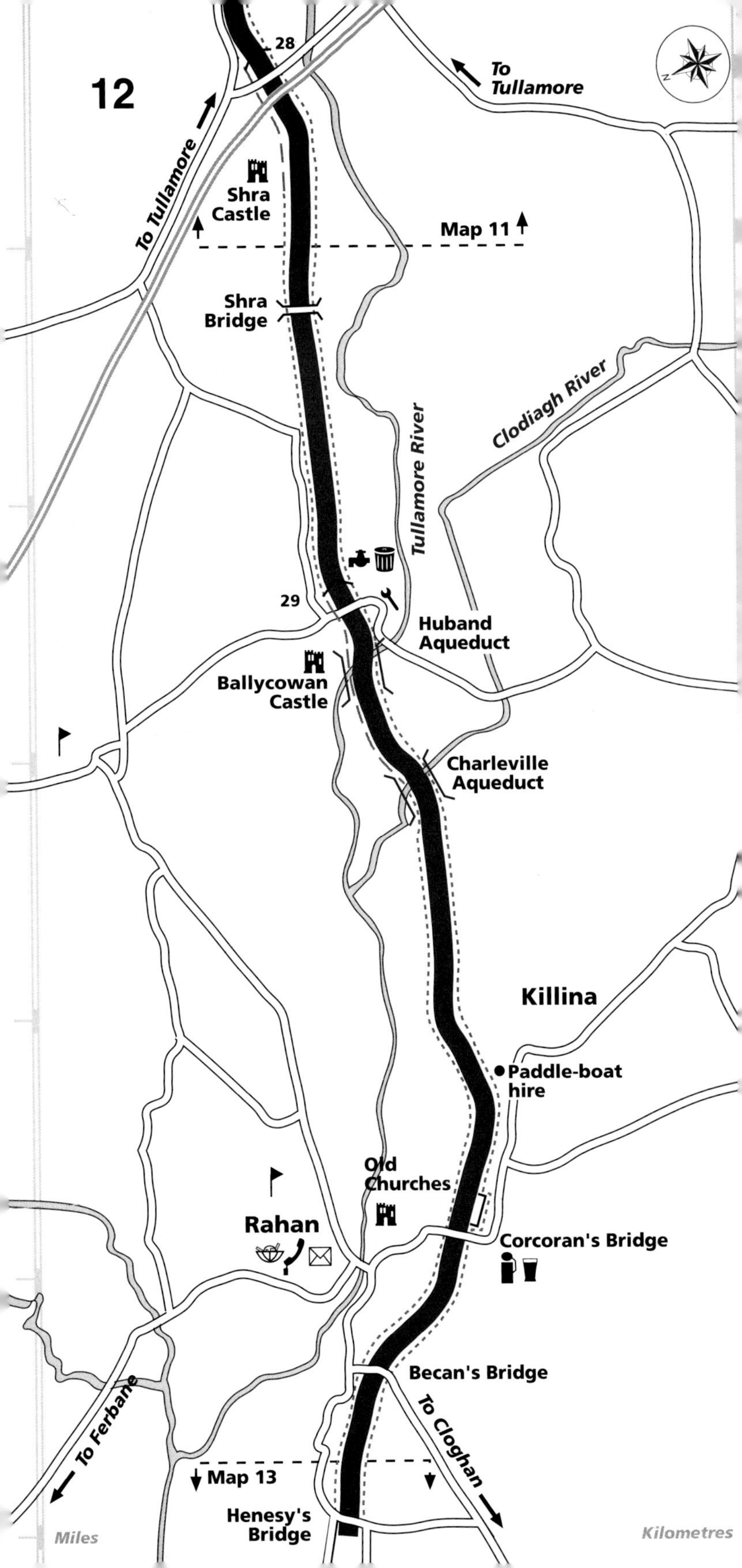
12
28
To Tullamore
To Tullamore
Shra Castle
Map 11
Shra Bridge
Clodiagh River
Tullamore River
29
Huband Aqueduct
Ballycowan Castle
Charleville Aqueduct
Killina
Paddle-boat hire
Old Churches
Rahan
Corcoran's Bridge
Becan's Bridge
To Ferbane
To Cloghan
Map 13
Henesy's Bridge
Miles
Kilometres

Tullamore to Henesy's Bridge, Rahan **12**

After passing under the Dublin-Athlone railway bridge, the canal curves around **Shra Castle,** passing an interesting old grave yard on the way to **Ballycowan.**

Just below **29th lock** the canal crosses the Tullamore River by the **Huband Aqueduct** and, close by, are the fine ruins of **Ballycowan Castle,** and a useful engineering works.

Rounding another bend, the canal crosses the Clodiagh River by the **Charleville Aqueduct**. A short distance west of the site of the old footbridge there is a quay where paddle boats and canoes can be hired. Further west is a convenient quay to moor while visiting **Rahan churches. Rahan** village lies a short distance to the north of the canal.

History **Shra Castle** was built by an Elizabethan officer, John Brisco, in 1588. **Ballycowan Castle**, built by Sir Jasper Herbert in 1626, is on the site of an earlier castle.

Huband Aqueduct is named after a prominent director, Joseph Huband, a barrister, who was elected in 1777 and, with the exception of a few years, remained a director until 1835. Lord Charleville was a prominent landowner. His castle lies to the south of the canal, built in 1801 to designs of Francis Johnston.

The Corcoran family were the owners of The Thatch and at one time Mr. Corcoran acted as agent to the company. In 1838 he reported that 350 passengers had used his station.

Rahan churches are attributed to St. Cartach. The largest, said to date from about 1100, is still used by the Church of Ireland. Its stone-roofed chancel was originally flanked by chambers; its arch and the unique circular east window are romanesque. The nave was rebuilt in the 18th century and the small church nearby is 15th century with a romanesque doorway. Other items of interest locally are the stained glass windows by Evie Hone at St.Stanislaus College, up until recently a Jesuit institution and now a nursing home.

Locks	29	8.1 ft fall	Overlapping Duties	Patricia Cummins lives at 29th lock Tel: (0506) 51 407

Facilities **Shop, Post-office:** Rahan, north from Becan's or Corcoran's Bridge.
Pub, Garage: near Corcoran's Bridge.
Water, Rubbish Disposal: Lock 29.

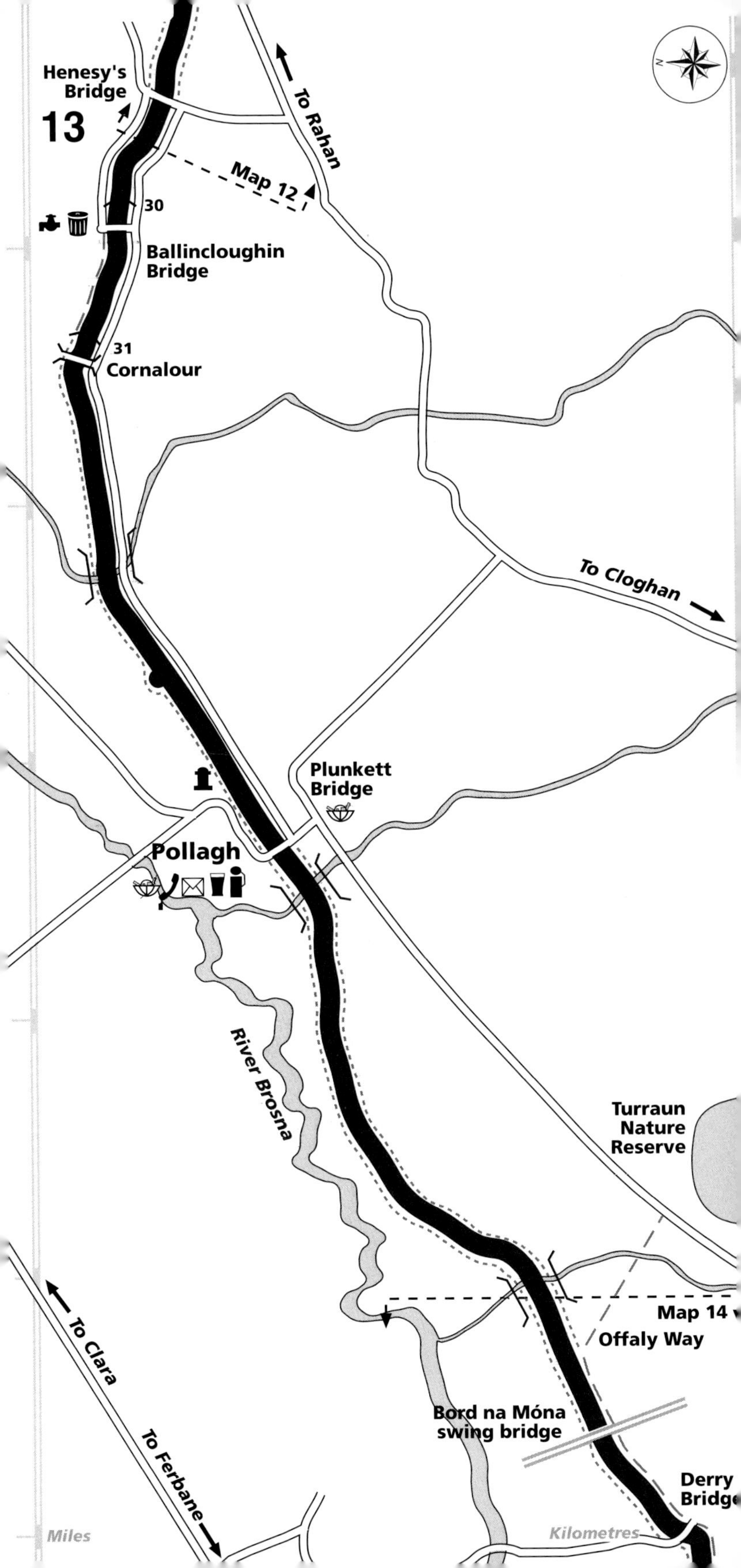

Henesy's Bridge
13
To Rahan
Map 12
30
Ballincloughin Bridge
31
Cornalour
To Cloghan
Plunkett Bridge
Pollagh
River Brosna
Turraun Nature Reserve
Map 14
Offaly Way
To Clara
Bord na Móna swing bridge
To Ferbane
Derry Bridge
Miles
Kilometres

Henesy's Bridge, Rahan to Derry Bridge 13

There is a quay below **31st lock** at **Cornalour** and then the canal swings around a corner to set off on a long level of nearly 10 miles (16 km). When travelling east, towards Dublin, it is easy to round this corner after the long level and meet the bridge and lock unexpectedly.

On the north bank just east of **Pollagh Bridge** is the best place to moor. **Pollagh,** with its quaint shaped church, has found a new prosperity with the Bord na Móna activity on the surrounding bogs and there are a number of new roads in the area. The church contains carvings and furniture made of bog oak, and is worth visiting.

West of **Pollagh** occasional glimpses of the River Brosna may be seen to the north. Drainage operations some years ago have left ugly mounds which indicate the presence of the river. The land between the river and the canal is scrub - poor agricultural land but rich in wildlife. To the south the extensive bog workings are apparent, with the twin towers of **Ferbane** power station visible to the west. Away to the south the **Slieve Bloom mountains** break the monotony of the flat country. The **Bord na Móna railway bridge** should be either manned or left open for boats.

History A glance at the map shows how closely the canal follows the River Brosna from Tullamore and it is interesting to note that Omer, the engineer who laid out the original line, planned to use the river. It was subsequently decided that a still-water navigation would be more practical.

Turraun peat works date back to the early 1900s and it was here that experiments were carried out in artificial methods of drying turf, but it was eventually decided that air-drying was the most efficient, and this is the method used today. The development of the bogs has brought about great changes in the area. A traveller along this stretch of canal in the 1830s described "the wretched hovels constructed of wet sods....the thatch is generally composed of rushes or stalks of the potato". Modern prosperity has long since swept such scenes away. The production of sod turf has ceased, and a nature reserve has been created from part of the cut-away bog at Turraun.

There is a local legend that St. Manchan cast a penance on the people of **Pollagh** to provide free milk to travellers because somebody stole his cow and put it in the pot. This custom survived to the days of the canal men but today's traveller will have to pay.

Locks			
	30	9.2 ft fall	Alan Lindley lives
	31	8.9 ft fall	at 30th lock
			Tel: (0506) 55 848

Facilities **Shops, Garage, Pub, Post-office:** Pollagh.
Water, Rubbish Disposal: Lock 30.

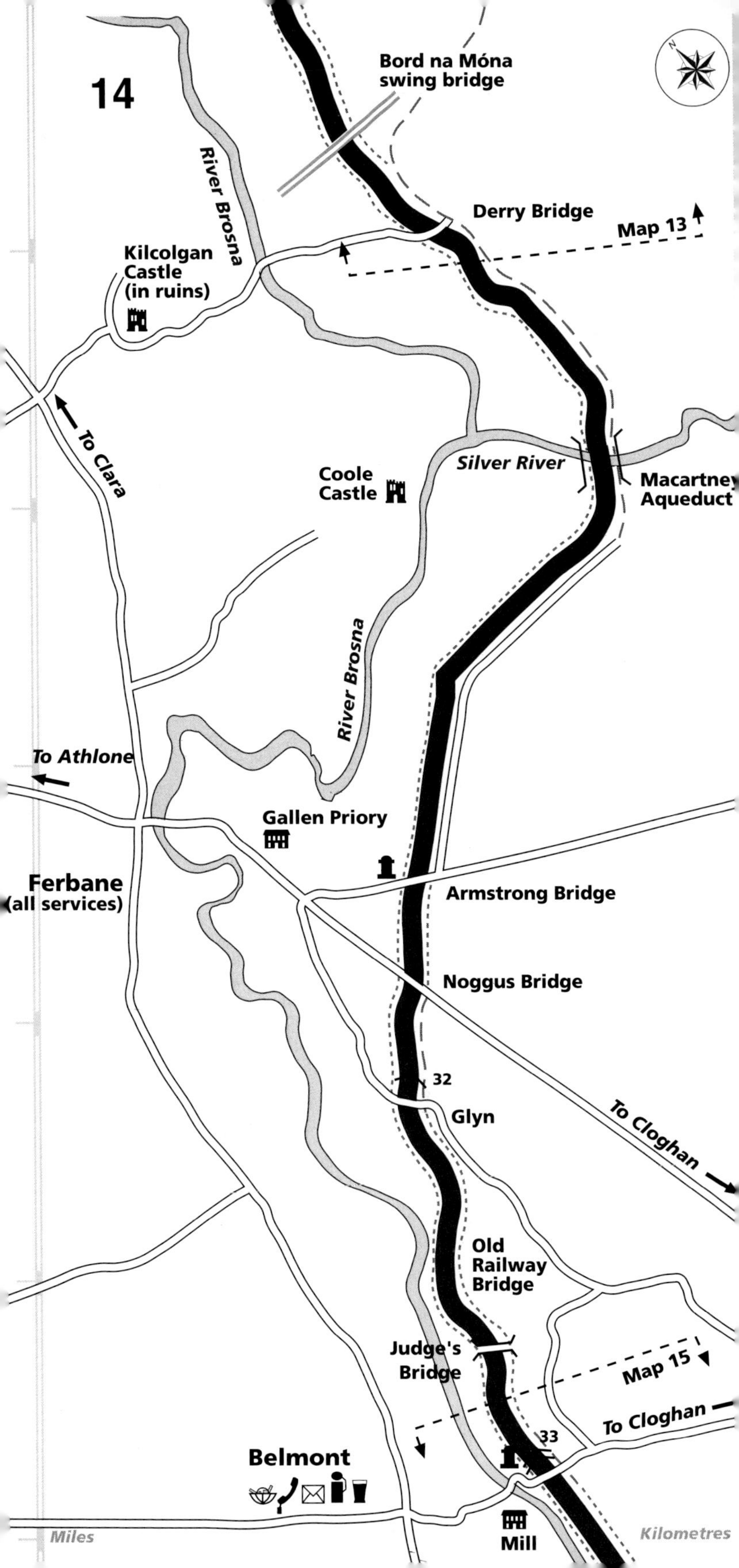
14
Bord na Móna
swing bridge
Derry Bridge
Map 13
River Brosna
Kilcolgan
Castle
(in ruins)
To Clara
Coole
Castle
Silver River
Macartney
Aqueduct
River Brosna
To Athlone
Gallen Priory
Ferbane
(all services)
Armstrong Bridge
Noggus Bridge
32
Glyn
To Cloghan
Old
Railway
Bridge
Judge's
Bridge
Map 15
To Cloghan
33
Belmont
Mill
Miles
Kilometres

Derry Bridge to Belmont

14

Because the canal curves around to cross the Silver River, there is an interesting view of **Macartney Aqueduct** in the distance.

There is an inspector's house and some old stables at **Armstrong Bridge**. West of the bridge there is a quay but the steps at the west end have collapsed making access difficult. From here the canal passes through a rock cutting to **Noggus Bridge,** another access point to **Ferbane.**

33rd lock is a double and is notoriously difficult to negotiate because the bridge is built across the lower chamber. A short distance to the north there is a fine bridge across the Brosna and the 18th-century Belmont mills, with the village of **Belmont** less than a mile (1.5 km) from the canal.

History

Kilcolgan Castle, a Jacobean strong-house of the MacCoughlan family, lies about 1.5 miles (2.5 km) to the north of **Derry Bridge**. The stones were taken for road materials and little remains but the bawn. **Coole Castle** is on the north bank of the Brosna almost due north from **Macartney Aqueduct**. It is a typical 15/16th century tower house with interesting angle loops and triple spiral ventilators.

The engineers had learnt from the earlier mistakes in cutting the canal through bog. A much longer time was allowed for subsidence here and the canal was carried through at the new level of the bog. There have been problems here, however, and a major canal breach occurred near **Derry Bridge** in January 1954, taking 4 months to repair.

Macartney Aqueduct, named after Sir John Macartney, the chairman of the board who was knighted at the opening of Ringsend Docks, proved a difficult piece of engineering for John Killaly, but it has stood the test of time well.

Gallen Priory is a gothicised Georgian house, formerly the home of the Armstrong family and now a convent. A monastery was founded here in the 5th century by St.Canoc, situated between the house and the river. In the middle ages it became an Augustinian priory and, although no traces of the buildings survive above ground, excavations have revealed a large number of grave slabs now mounted in the rebuilt gable wall of the excavated church. To the south across the river are the ruins of a 15th-century parish church which lay outside the monastery.

Locks			
	32	9.6 ft fall	Alan Wynne
	33 (double)	15.9 ft fall	based at 33rd lock
			Tel: (0902) 57 284

Facilities

All Services: Ferbane, 2 miles (3 km) north from Armstrong Bridge;
Shops, Garage, Pubs, Post-office: Belmont, 1 mile (1.5 km) north from 33rd lock.

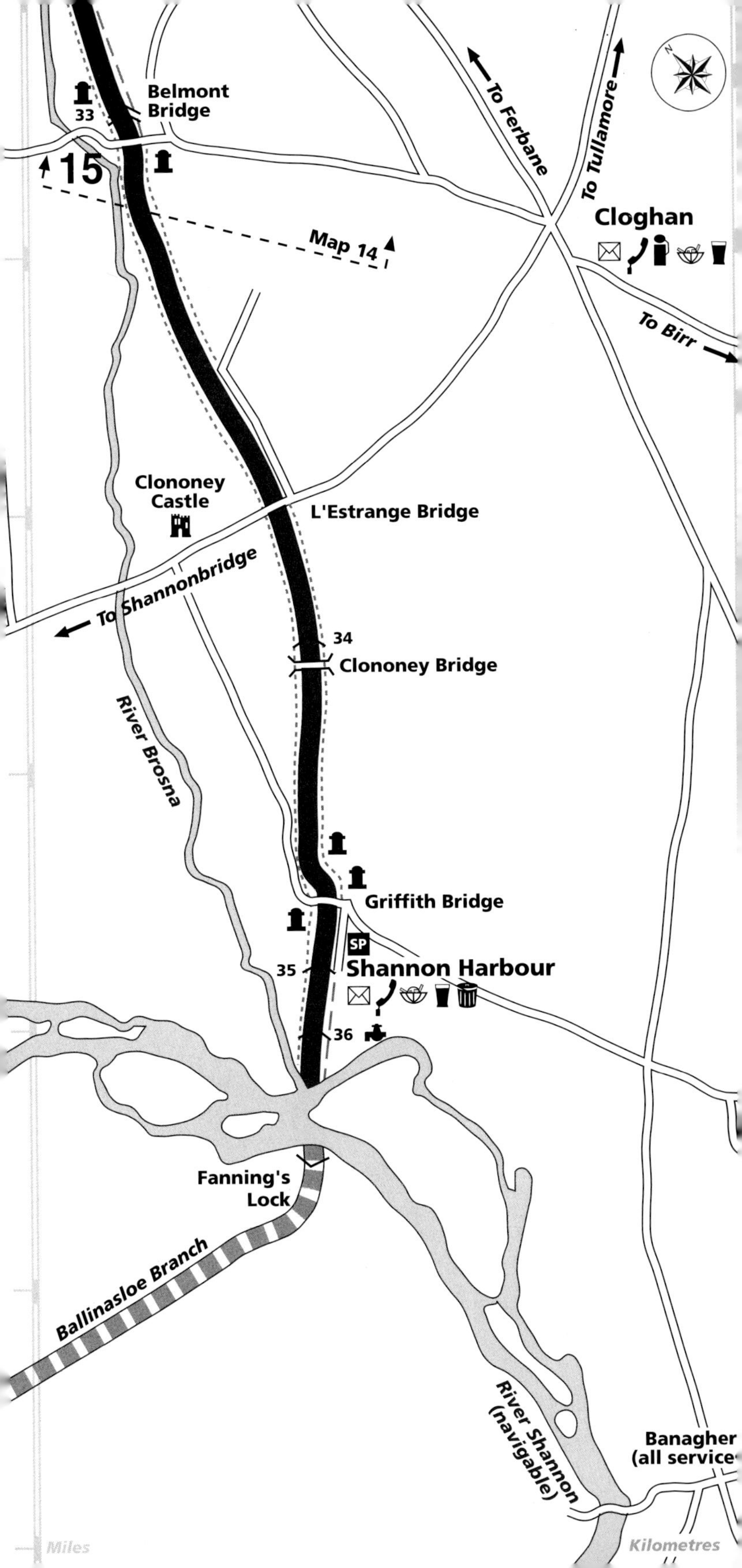

Belmont
Bridge
33
15
Map 14
To Ferbane
To Tullamore
Cloghan
To Birr
Clononey
Castle
L'Estrange Bridge
To Shannonbridge
34
Clononey Bridge
River Brosna
Griffith Bridge
SP
35
Shannon Harbour
36
Fanning's
Lock
Ballinasloe Branch
River Shannon
(navigable)
Banagher
(all service
Miles
Kilometres

Belmont to Shannon Harbour

15

From **Belmont** to **L'Estrange Bridge** the canal is hemmed in by bushes. This level used to get rather shallow, because boats locking in and out of Shannon Harbour drew off the water. Now, during dry summers, water is back-pumped from the Shannon.

Griffith Bridge, bearing the rope marks of earlier years, is at the entrance to **Shannon Harbour**. Here one is very conscious of the past with the old hotel, buildings and warehouses. There is a jetty below **36th lock.** The Brosna, entering the Shannon here, causes heavy silting, and the deep channel is near the south bank. Travelling downstream on the Shannon, it is possible to mistake the entrance to the canal, which is to the south of the small island. **Fanning's Lock,** the entrance to the **Ballinasloe Branch,** is across the river. This branch line is now closed and much of it has disappeared in bog working.

History

At **L'Estrange Bridge** are the ruins of a former inn. A short distance up the road to the north, there are large gates which led to a former military barracks, now demolished - one of a series built in the early 1800s to meet the threat of French invasion from the west. About 0.5 mile (less than 1 km) from the bridge along the same road is **Clononey Castle**. It has a well preserved bawn and a 16th-century tower house, which was restored in the last century by an eccentric lawyer. There is an interesting grave slab here, bearing the names of some of the Boleyn family, which is said to have been unearthed by workmen quarrying stone for the canal works.

The canal was completed in 1803 but considerable difficulty was experienced in staunching parts of it. A boat did pass through in April 1804, but it was not until 1805 that the link was permanently secured. The hotel at **Shannon Harbour** was completed in 1806, but was only successful for a short period when emigrants were making their way to the New World. The agent's house, a police barracks and some of the old warehouses remain.
In 1946 the new loading shed was built and **35th** and **36th locks** were enlarged (85ft x 16ft). It is difficult to believe it now, but the harbour area was once bustling with activity, and large numbers of people were employed in various boat-related businesses.

The Ballinasloe Branch (14.5 miles (23 km) long with 2 locks) was completed in 1828 and the remains of the old horse bridge across the Shannon are still visible. It was replaced by a ferry in 1849, which was abandoned when the boats were mechanised.

Locks

34	8.7 ft fall	Jason Pender lives at
35	6.1 ft fall	35th lock
36	variable	Tel: (0509) 51 163

Facilities

All Services: Banagher.
Shops, Garage, Pubs, Post-office: Cloghan.
Shops, Pubs, Post-office, Water: Shannon Harbour.
Water, Rubbish Disposal: Lock 35.

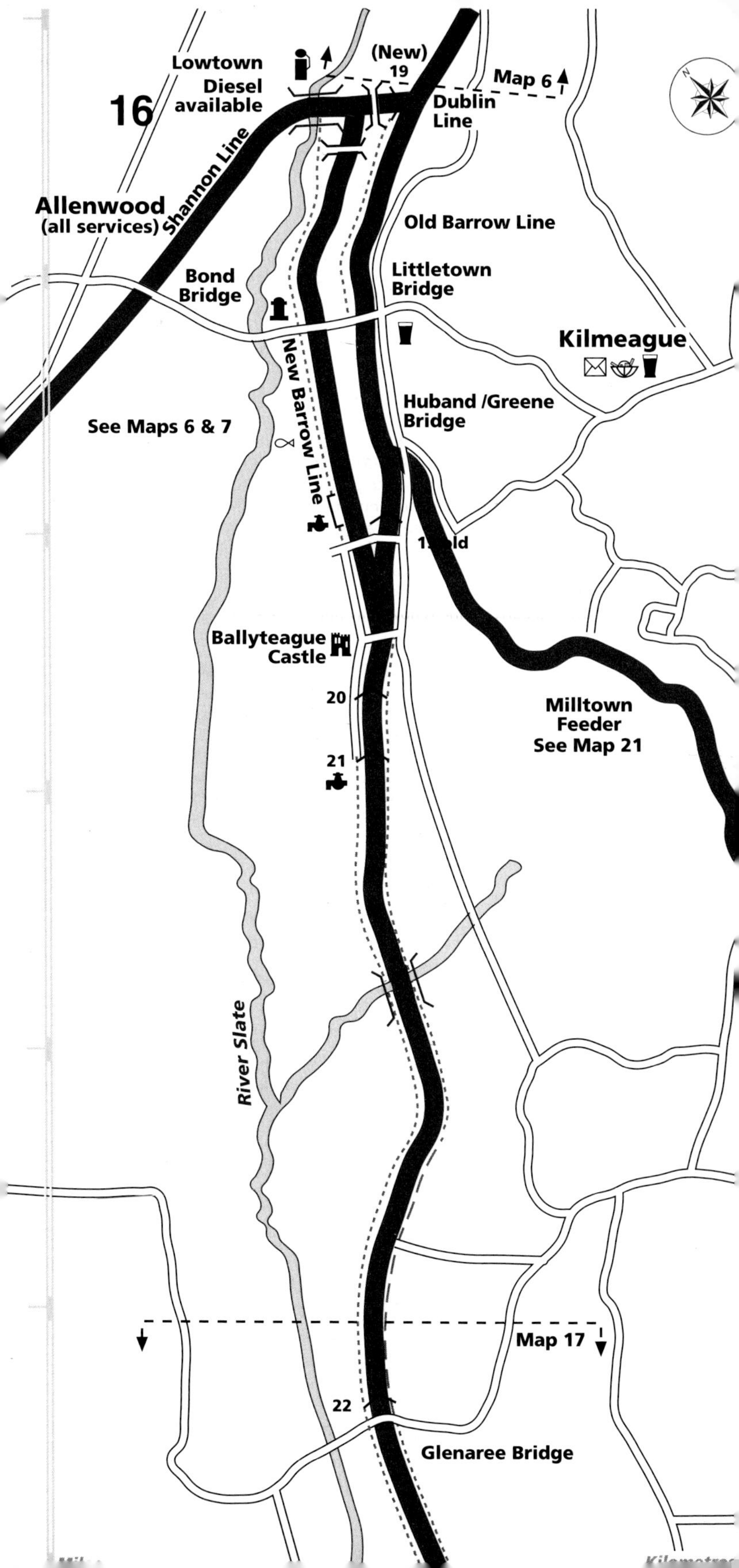
16
Lowtown
Diesel
available
(New)
19
Map 6
Dublin
Line
Shannon Line
Allenwood
(all services)
Old Barrow Line
Littletown
Bridge
Bond
Bridge
Kilmeague
New Barrow Line
Huband /Greene
Bridge
See Maps 6 & 7
Ballyteague
Castle
20
21
Milltown
Feeder
See Map 21
River Slate
Map 17
22
Glenaree Bridge

Lowtown to Glenaree

16

The Barrow Line of the Grand Canal joins the Main Line a short distance below **19th lock**. The **Milltown Feeder** is navigable by shallow draught boats requiring limited headroom (map 21).

Passing down through **20th** and **21st locks** the canal crosses Ballyteague Bog and it is very exposed here in windy weather.

History The bridge over the **Milltown Feeder** near the old **19th lock** presents a puzzle. On one side it bears the inscription **Huband Bridge 1788** and on the other face **Greene Bridge 1799.** Joseph Huband was one of the canal directors and Greene was an early secretary of the company.

The old Barrow Line, into which the **Milltown Feeder** flows, was the original line of the canal. In 1804 the new Barrow Line was constructed to save water. This became the only route with the closure of the **old 19th lock** in the 1860s. The old line was re-opened in 1973 to provide a circular route for local boats. Unfortunately the problems solved by the building of the new Barrow Line reappeared when the old line was opened again, and it had to be closed just ten years later, for exactly the same reasons as it had been 120 years previously. However the old 19th lock has been re-opened once more, and the Old Barrow Line is now fully navigable again.

Just north of the jetty at Ballyteague, on the New Barrow Line, there is a line of angling stands. Some of these were designed specifically for use by people with disabilities, and allow easy and safe access for wheelchair users to fish the canal. **Ballyteague Castle** is a typical example of the Irish fortified house of the fourteenth to sixteenth century. It is thought to have been a Geraldine Castle and Silken Thomas is said to have taken refuge here after the battle of Allen in 1535.

To the east is the **Hill of Allen** (676 ft./203 metres) where Finn MacCool is reputed to have lived. The tower is a folly erected about 1860 by one of the Aylmer family on the site of a pre-historic tumulus.

The canal through Ballyteague Bog proved very difficult to construct and severe bog subsidence eventually forced the canal company to construct a new stretch of canal. **21st lock**, which was originally at the southern end of the bog near the aqueduct was removed, **20th lock** became **21st** at a lower level and a new lock was inserted, the present **20th**. All signs of the old line have now disappeared but the lowering of the **21st lock** is apparent from the lock-house which is sitting up on its original foundations.

Locks			
	19 Main Line	7.9 ft fall	James Conroy 19th lock, Lowtown Tel: (045) 860 237
	19 Old Barrow Line	7.9 ft fall	Peter Goulding 19 Lock, Old Barrow Line
	20 Ballyteague 21 Ballyteague	6.2 ft fall 7.0 ft fall	Michael Murphy lives at 20th lock Tel: (045) 860 725
	22 Glenaree	10.0 ft fall	P.J. Donegan lives near 23rd lock Tel: (045) 524 270

Facilities **All Services:** Allenwood.
Shops, Pubs, Post-office: Robertstown; Kilmeague.
Pub: Littletown Bridge, Milltown Feeder.

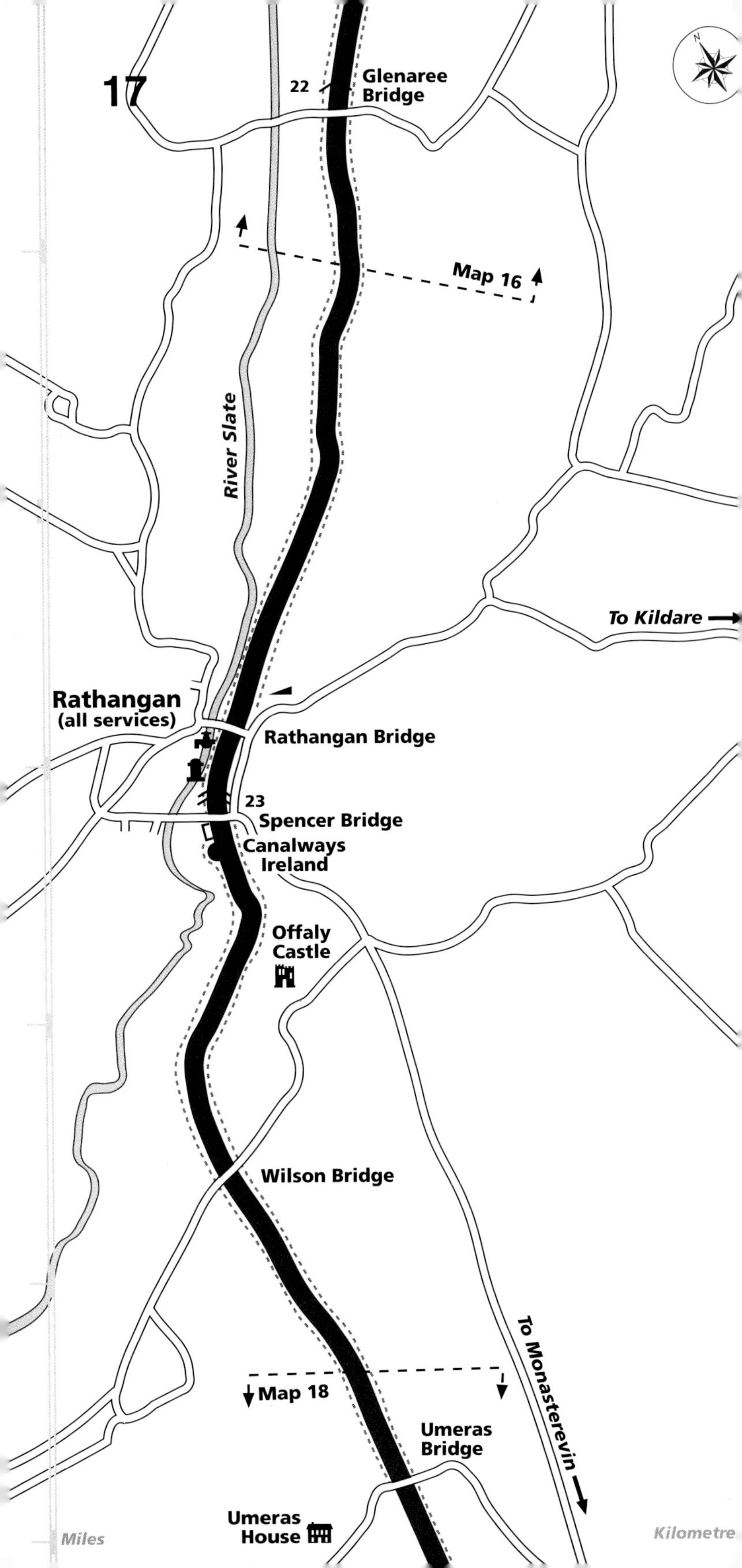
17
22
Glenaree Bridge
Map 16
River Slate
To Kildare
Rathangan
(all services)
Rathangan Bridge
23
Spencer Bridge
Canalways Ireland
Offaly Castle
Wilson Bridge
To Monasterevin
Map 18
Umeras Bridge
Umeras House
Miles
Kilometre

Glenaree to Umeras

17

Once through **Glenaree Bridge** the canal becomes more sheltered and some afforestation has been carried out. The spire of Rathangan church is clearly visible in the distance. The attractive old warehouses at the approach to **Rathangan** were destroyed by fire some years ago but the local people have made great efforts to improve the waterfront and there is convenient mooring between the bridges with good shopping facilities. The old harbour below the double lock is an indication that this was once a busy canal centre. There is now a hire-boat base, Canalways Ireland, below 23rd lock and Spencer Bridge. The Slate River, known as the Little Barrow below Rathangan Bridge, closes with the canal here and the ugly mounds raised when this river was dredged may be seen to the west.

Just north of **Rathangan** the canal is carried on an embankment above the level of the surrounding countryside. At the base of the embankment on both sides of the canal there are small areas of wetland, where many plant species rare elsewhere along the canal system can grow - including Grass-of-Parnassus and a number of different orchids.

History

The early engineers experienced difficulty with this stretch of canal as well as the bog section. Mistakes in the levels forced the company to turn **Rathangan lock** into a double lock. Local contractors were employed under the supervision of the company engineer and there is a noticeable difference in the quality of the materials used in some of the bridges.

The ancient rath, an imposing 180 ft (54 metres) in diameter, from which **Rathangan** takes its name, is still visible but Rathangan Castle was demolished in the 1760s. In the records of the company there is a mention of the purchasing of land for the canal from James Spencer of Rathangan House in 1784. In 1798 the same Mr.Spencer was piked to death in his house by insurgents but his name survives on the bridge. Two days later the insurgents under John Doorley were driven from the town and Doorley was killed. His death is recorded on the family tombstone in the local churchyard.

South of **Spencer Bridge** on the east bank there is a good example of a canal milestone. In 1783 the board ordered milestones in English miles (1760 yards/1609 metres) from James's Street Harbour to be placed on the north (or west) bank and in Irish miles (2240 yards/2048 metres) from Dublin Castle on the south (or east) bank.

A peat litter factory was set up at **Umeras** in 1885 attempting to utilise some of the turf in the area. Amongst other things experiments were tried in producing board from turf but without success. The factory continued under different owners until it was destroyed by fire in1940 and today the remains of a quay and a few mooring posts are all that survive of this industrial activity.

Locks 23 (double) 17.2 ft fall

P.J. Donegan lives near 23rd lock
Tel: (045) 524 270

Facilities **All Services:** Rathangan.
Slip: Rathangan Bridge.

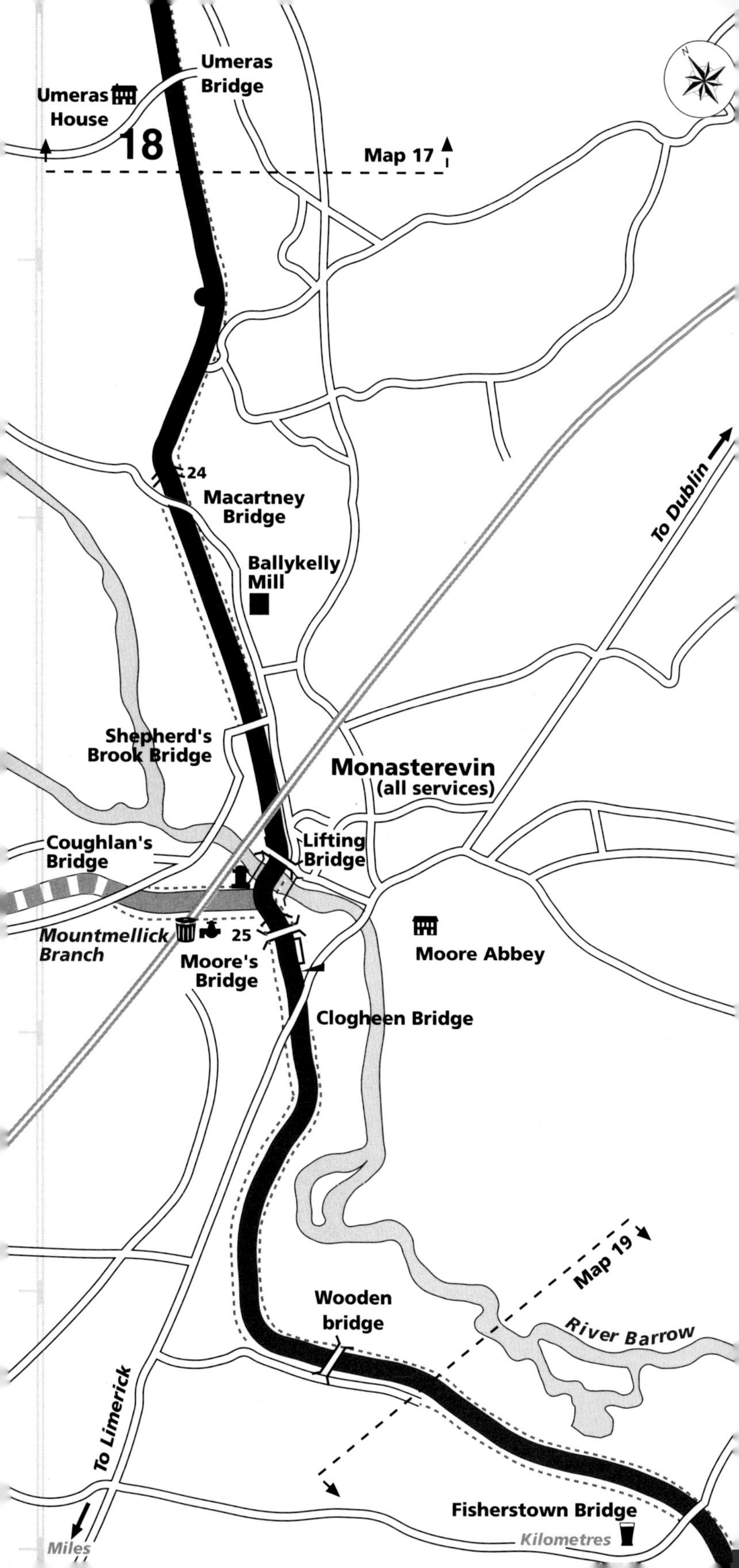

Umeras Bridge
Umeras House
18
Map 17
24
Macartney Bridge
Ballykelly Mill
To Dublin
Shepherd's Brook Bridge
Monasterevin
(all services)
Coughlan's Bridge
Lifting Bridge
Mountmellick Branch
25
Moore's Bridge
Moore Abbey
Clogheen Bridge
Map 19
Wooden bridge
River Barrow
To Limerick
Fisherstown Bridge
Miles
Kilometres

Umeras to Fisherstown

18

Macartney Bridge and double lock form an attractive scene with whitewashed cottages. Passing Ballykelly Mill, founded in 1801, the canal approaches **Monasterevin** with its maze of waterways, roads and railways and its multiplicity of bridges ancient and modern. One of these, an interesting old lifting bridge over the canal, must be opened before proceeding. In order to open the bridge the lock-keeper **must be summoned from 24th or 25th lock.** Crossing the River Barrow by a fine aqueduct with three 40 ft (12 metre) spans, the canal turns to the south while the Mountmellick Branch, now derelict, veers off to the west. It is possible to walk to the first bridge over the branch, known locally as **Coughlan's Bridge** after a family who lived nearby. Emerging from the **25th lock** and **Moore's Bridge,** the canal turns sharply and this bend can present problems when travelling towards Dublin with the bridge and lock appearing unexpectedly. Passing behind an old charter school building, the canal approaches a new road bridge carrying the main road from Dublin to Limerick and Cork.

The canal now follows the line of the Barrow valley and there is a long level of 13 miles (21 km) ahead.

History Attention often focuses on the various ways of spelling Monasterevin, even among the local people. Some say the town derives its name from a monastery founded here by St. Evin. The site of the ancient monastery is now occupied by **Moore Abbey,** built in 1607 and enlarged in 1846. For many years it was the seat of the Moores, Earls of Drogheda, and was subsequently the home of John Count McCormack before being purchased by the Sisters of Charity.

There is a wealth of local history connected with this town which was once the centre of several thriving industries, including Cassidy's distillery (1784-1934). A short branch canal formerly ran into the centre of the town and the old harbour area may still be traced. Two small harbours on the west side of the canal have now been filled in but some of the attractive old buildings remain, among them a well preserved three-story house which was once a canal hotel.

It was originally intended that the navigation should enter the River Barrow here but it was subsequently decided to continue the still-water canal to Athy. In the early years the boats used to lock down into the river and up on the far side and the blind bridge near the lifting bridge and the sites of these early locks are still visible. However, when the **Mountmellick Branch** was constructed in the 1820s, it was decided to do away with this unsatisfactory arrangement and the aqueduct and lifting bridge were erected. The Mountmellick Branch had originally been envisaged as a canal to the Castlecomer coal fields but all that was accomplished was the 11 miles (18 km) to Mountmellick. By the 1950s it had almost ceased to be used and it was officially closed to navigation in 1960. The land was sold off, and many stretches, including the section through **Portarlington,** have now been filled in, so there is little hope of restoring this branch.

Locks	24 (double)	12.8 ft fall	Peter Moore
	25	9.0 ft fall	lives at 25th lock
			Tel: (045) 525 275
			(087) 247 3093

Facilities **All Services:** Monasterevin.

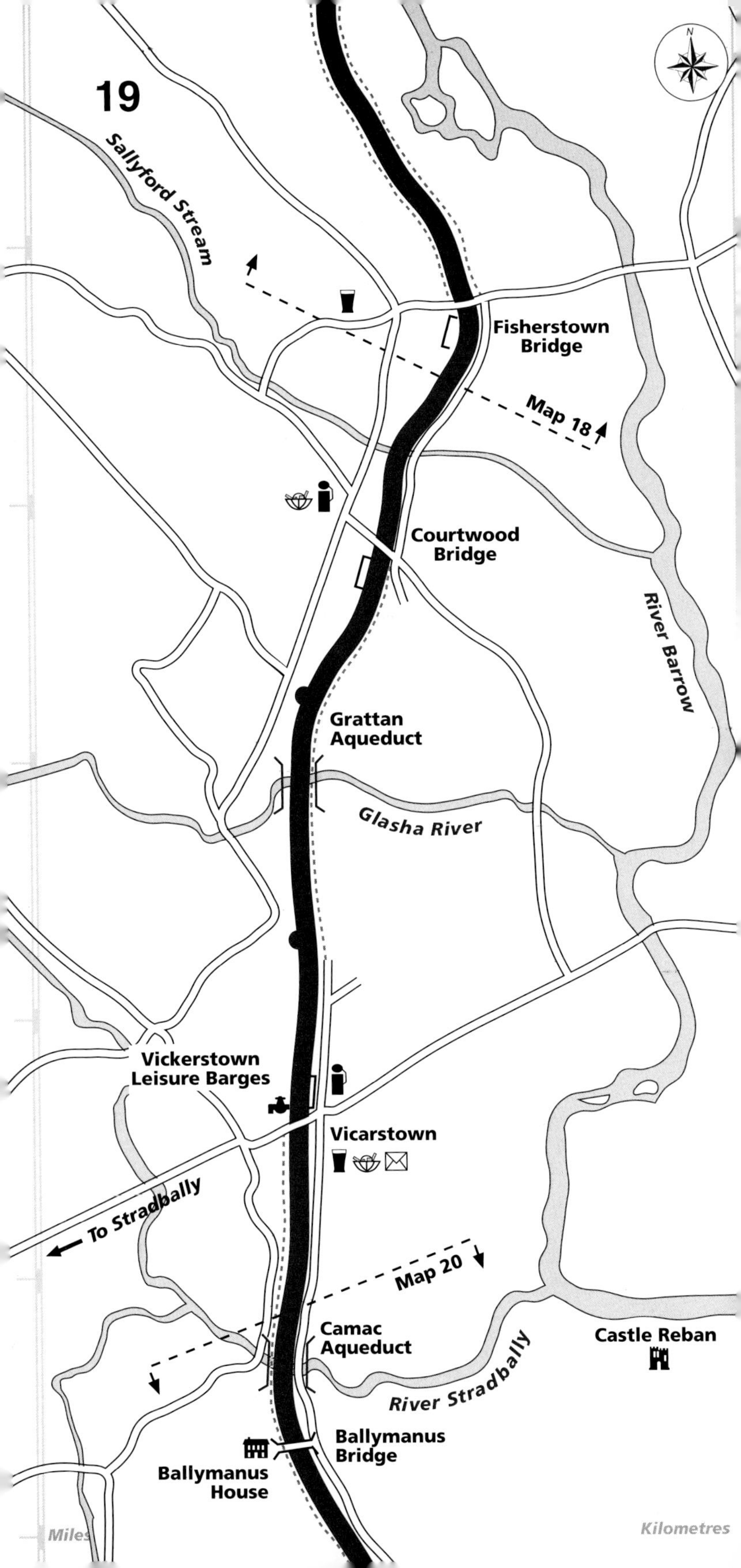
19
Sallyford Stream
Fisherstown Bridge
Map 18
Courtwood Bridge
River Barrow
Grattan Aqueduct
Glasha River
Vickerstown Leisure Barges
Vicarstown
To Stradbally
Map 20
Camac Aqueduct
Castle Reban
River Stradbally
Ballymanus Bridge
Ballymanus House
Miles
Kilometres

Fisherstown Bridge to Ballymanus Bridge **19**

In order to achieve the Long Level without a lock the canal is now carried on an embankment to **Fisherstown Bridge** and then through a cutting to **Courtwood Bridge.** **Vicarstown** is an attractive village with friendly pubs on both sides of the canal. From here it is possible to walk about 1 mile (1.5 km) to the east to Dunrally Castle and Bridge over the Barrow and the more energetic travellers might like to go to Stradbally 4 miles (5 km) to the west where there is an interesting steam museum. There is a road along the canal all the way from Vicarstown to Athy.

History

The canal from Monasterevin to Athy was constructed in the same way as the Main Line, with the work divided up into lots to be undertaken by local contractors. It was not until some time later that the larger canal contractors emerged, but it is interesting that one of the local contractors on this stretch was John McMahon, co-founder of the first large civil engineering firm in this country. Both his partners, Bernard Mullins and David Henry, also started as small contractors working on the Grand Canal. Together, as Henry, Mullins and McMahon, they were responsible for the construction of the Naas Branch of the Grand Canal from Naas to Corbally Harbour, the Ballinasloe and Mountmellick Branches, also part of the Grand Canal network, and for the Royal Canal from Coolnahay, west of Mullingar, to Richmond Harbour and the Shannon.

At one time there were over 4,000 men at work on the Barrow Line. Again there were troubles with inaccurate surveys which caused errors in the levels. Omer's original estimate for the canal from Dublin to Athy had been £98,000 and the final cost was just under half a million pounds.

Ballymanus Bridge is heavily scored with rope marks made by the horse-drawn boats of the past as they turned the corner into the bridge. Where the canal bends towards the River Barrow, Castle Reban is visible with Bert House on the nearby hill. Castle Reban was a thirteenth-century castle built on the site of an ancient town according to Ptolemy's map of the second century. Fynes Moryson, the famous traveller, passing through here in 1617 remarked, "I pass over...the ancient city of Reban, now a poor village with a castle". Today there is not even a village remaining and there is a private house beside the ruined castle.

Facilities

Shops, Pubs, Post-office, Garage: Vicarstown.
Pub: Fisherstown Bridge, about 200 yards (200 m) to the west of the bridge.
Shop and Garage: about 0.25 mile (0.5 km) west of Courtwood Quay.

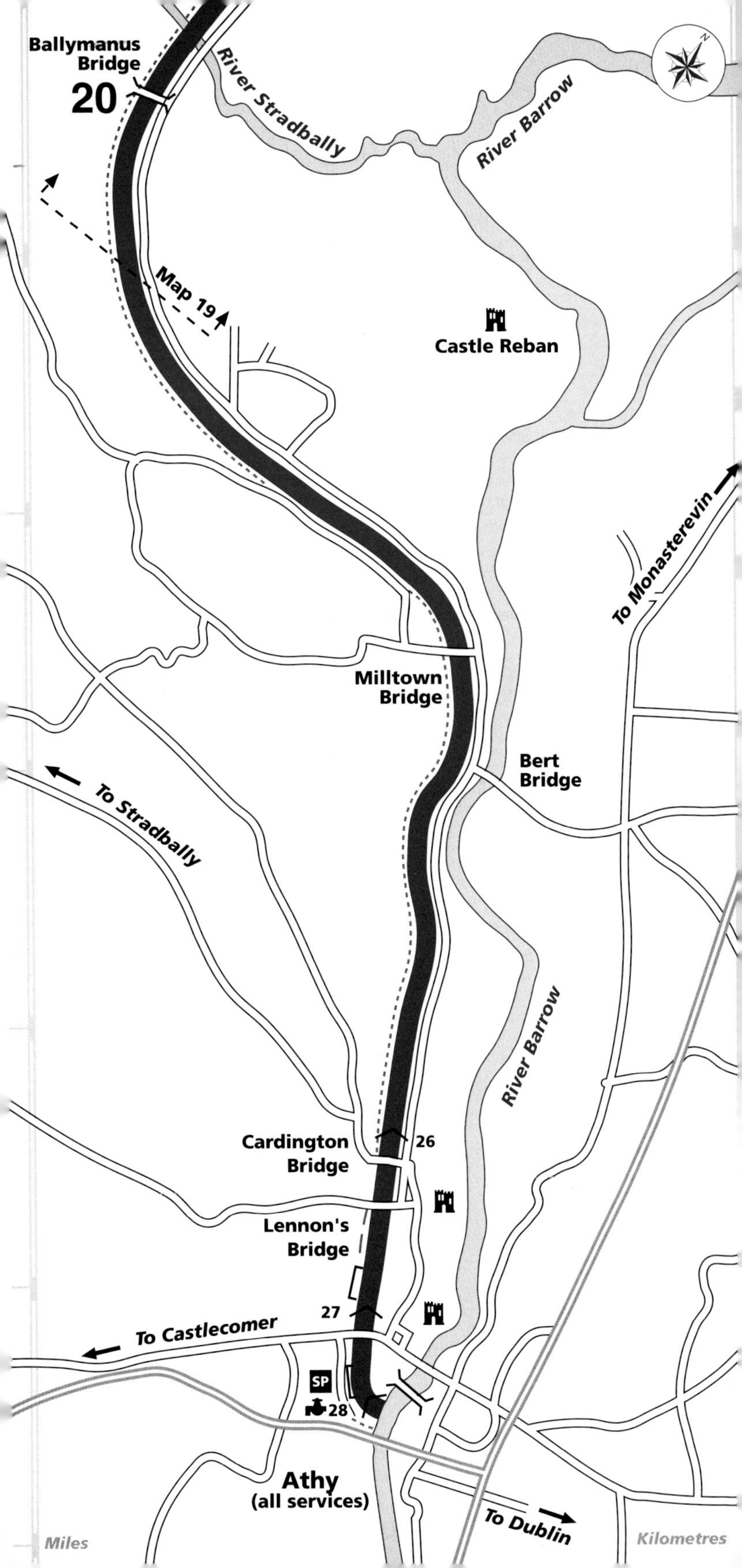
Ballymanus Bridge
20
River Stradbally
River Barrow
Map 19
Castle Reban
To Monasterevin
Milltown Bridge
Bert Bridge
To Stradbally
River Barrow
Cardington Bridge
26
Lennon's Bridge
27
To Castlecomer
SP
28
Athy (all services)
To Dublin
Miles
Kilometres

Ballymanus Bridge to Athy

20

Glimpses of the Barrow increase as the canal and river near their junction at **Athy.** In places the accompanying road swings slightly away from the canal creating an impression of isolation. There is a good view of the town as the canal drops down to the river level. Here the canal opens out into a harbour, and while this is a convenient place to moor for shopping, it should be remembered that it is never a good idea to leave a boat unattended in the larger towns.

Before locking out through **28th lock** into the river, it is well worth looking at the attractive horse bridge spanning the river here. From it, looking upstream, there is a good view of the town with the interesting Dominican church with a paraboloid roof, erected in 1965. The river is navigable up to the town bridge but there are obstructions in the water at the old quay and it is better to moor near the new church. Looking downstream the first of the river navigation's unguarded weirs may be seen beneath the railway bridge and on the east bank the entrance to the first of the navigation cuts. On emerging from the lock it is necessary to cross the river to enter this cut.

History From early times small boats have used the Barrow above Athy and even after the canal was completed they continued to do so to avoid the payment of tolls. There is evidence that at one time there was a lock just above Athy.

Athy (the ford of Ae) has been an important river crossing from early times and is full of historical interest. It has been the site of many battles from the time in the eleventh century when Ae, King of Leinster, fell here. In 1308 the town was burned by the native Irish and seven years later it was again plundered, this time by the Scots under Robert Bruce. The town bridge was built in 1796 but the first recorded bridge on this site dates back to 1413. Beside the bridge is **White's Castle**, which was built in 1506 by the eighth Earl of Kildare. Seventy years later it was enlarged by William White, hence its name. A short distance upstream is **Woodstock Castle,** built in the thirteenth century and later taken over by the Fitzgeralds. According to tradition Thomas, the infant son of Maurice Fitzjohn, was rescued by a monkey when there was a fire in this castle and thereafter there has always been a monkey in the Kildare coat-of-arms.

Locks			
	26	11.25 ft fall	Noel Cross
	27	9.3 ft fall	28th Lock House
	28	8.5 ft fall (variable)	Tel: (0507) 38 488

Facilities **All Services:** Athy.
Slip: Athy, in river, upstream of Dublin Road Bridge.
Pump-out Station: Athy.

Barrow Navigation

Before proceeding downstream, it is essential to obtain a copy of *The Guide to the Barrow Navigation* because there are many hazards. It is a river navigation with side canals and the boat-stream changes sides in a number of places.

21
Harberton Bridge
19 Old
20
21
Barrow Line
Littletown
Bridge
Map 6
Huband /
Greene
Bridge
NAVIGATION
WARNING
SEE TEXT
Kilmeague
Pim Bridge
To Rathangan
Pluckerstown Bridge
(6'0" clearance)
Hill of Allen
676'
Milltown
To Newbridge
Point of
Gibraltar
POLLARDSTOWN
FEN
Fr. Moore's
Well

Navigation Warning

The maximum size of craft that can navigate the Milltown Feeder is limited to 2ft 6in (0.75m) draught and 6ft (1.8m) height over water-line due to restricted clearance at Pluckerstown Bridge. It is not possible to turn a craft of more than 25ft (7.5m) at Pluckerstown. The limit of navigation is the Point of Gibraltar where there is ample room to turn.

The Milltown Feeder

The Milltown Feeder, or as it is sometimes called, The Grand Supply, is the main source of water for the Grand Canal, entering the summit level above the old 19th lock near **Lowtown**. Passing close to the village of **Kilmeague** it follows the natural contour around the **Hill of Allen** to **Milltown Bridge,** a total distance of about 6 miles (10 km) from Lowtown. It continues into Pollardstown Fen, a further 2 miles (3 km) to the Seven Springs, narrowing as it approaches the small pool with its bubbling springs of crystal clear water, also known as James's Well. In the late eighteenth century further supplies were added to the main supply, drawing from the western side of the fen, an area around Father Moore's Well. There are 36 known springs in the whole area. There were originally three mills, at **Pollardstown, Milltown** and **Pluckerstown,** also drawing on this excellent supply and so the whole area is most confusing with old millraces, streams and drains, some natural and some artificial.

The Feeder, because of its proximity with the **Curragh** and the military camps there, was used from time to time both by cargo and passenger boats as far as **Milltown Bridge**.

In the late 1970s the future of the Fen and the Canal's water supply was threatened by proposed drainage schemes by the local landowners. Following public protest, the government agreed to preserve the Fen and it is now a nature reserve.

Pollardstown Fen

The Fen is of particular botanical interest because it represents the unique survival of a type of landscape and vegetation which was widespread throughout the country some 5000 years ago. Fens gradually evolved from shallow lakes but most of them subsequently became covered by raised bogland. Pollardstown survived because the great quantities of lime-rich alkaline waters from the springs preserved the water table and retained the right conditions for it to remain as a fen.

Pollardstown Fen contains many different plants and vegetation types, some rare and others less so - including Saw-sedge, Black Bog-rush, Purple Moor-grass, Common Reed, Fen Rush, Fen Bog-cotton, Fen Sedge, Hemp Agrimony, Angelica and Fen Thistle. Of particular interest are the insectivorous plants (Butterwort and Bladderwort) and the orchids (Fragrant Orchid, Fly Orchid and the Marsh Orchids).

The Fen provides a habitat for many wildfowl and insects and is home of a small rare snail *(Vertigo geyeri).*

Visitors should not wander about the Fen - it can be very dangerous because of the wet ground and many deep drains. The removal of any living or non-living things from the Fen is strictly forbidden.

Facilities **Shop, Pub:** Kilmeague; Milltown.
Pub: Littletown Bridge.

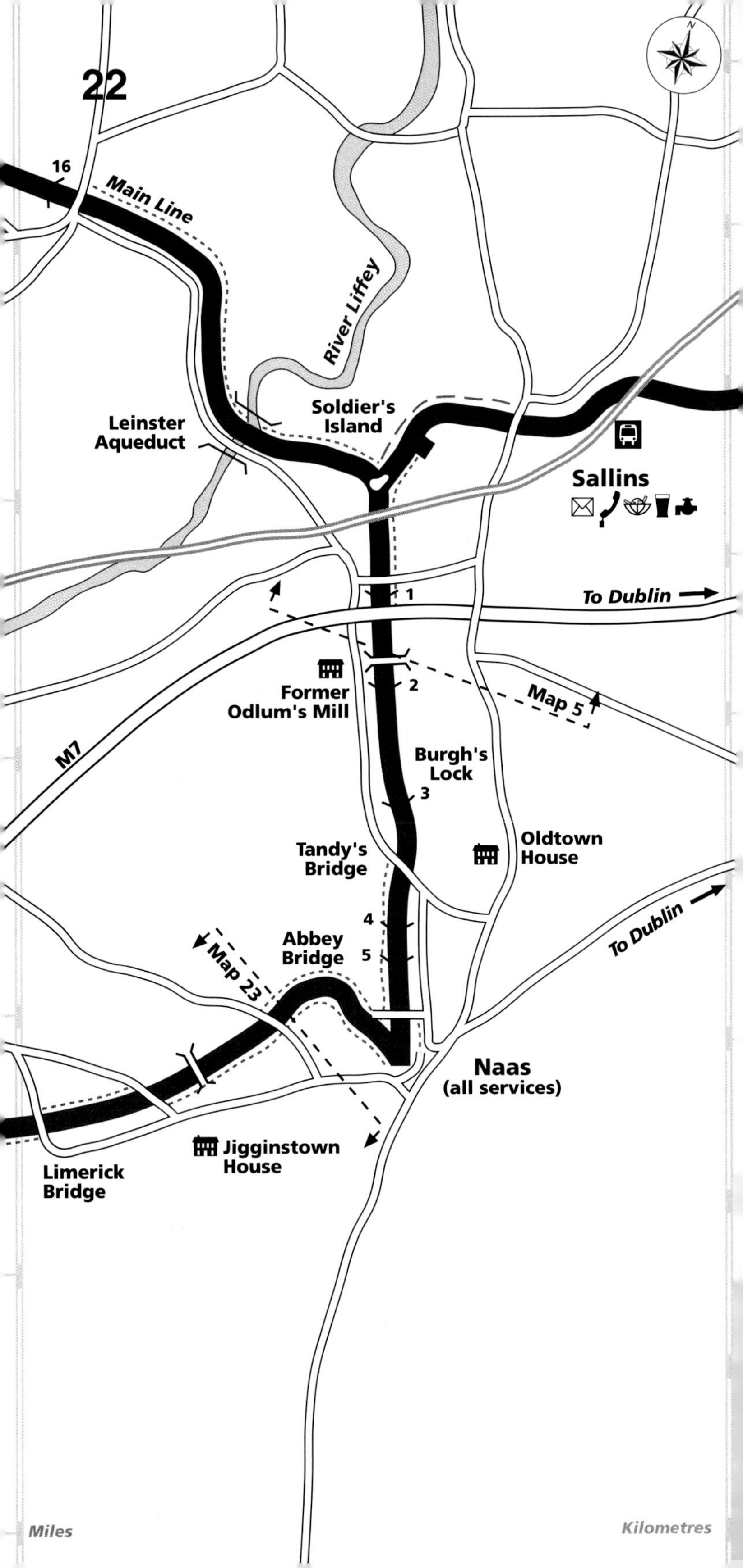
22
16
Main Line
River Liffey
Leinster
Aqueduct
Soldier's
Island
Sallins
1
To Dublin
2
Former
Odlum's Mill
Map 5
M7
Burgh's
Lock
3
Tandy's
Bridge
Oldtown
House
4
Abbey
Bridge
5
Map 23
To Dublin
Naas
(all services)
Jigginstown
House
Limerick
Bridge
Miles
Kilometres

The Naas and Corbally Branch Soldier's Island to Naas Harbour

22

The Naas Branch enters the Main Line of the canal at **Soldier's Island,** between **Sallins** and **Leinster Aqueduct** (Map 5). It extends southwards for about 2.5 miles (4 km) to **Naas Harbour** and is a most attractive stretch of waterway surrounded by woodland and lined by fine beech trees. It is possible to drive along the canal for almost its entire length. Between **1st lock, Osbertstown Bridge**, and **2nd lock** at Odlum's Mills the canal is crossed by the motorway which by-passes Naas. It continues on through **Burgh lock** and **Tandy's Bridge** at Oldtown, past the old Naas gasworks between **4th** and **5th locks,** before passing under **Abbey** (or Finlay) **Bridge** to enter the harbour at **Naas.**

History

The County of Kildare Canal Company was set up in 1786 by local landowners to construct a canal to Naas. The canal was completed in 1789 and work was commenced on an extension to Kilcullen and Co. Wicklow, but the company was heavily in debt and entered into negotiations with the Grand Canal Company to sell out. No agreement was reached and eventually, in 1807, the Grand Canal Company bought the concern from the Court of Chancery for a mere £2,250. The three Naas Canal bridges were rebuilt with increased headroom. This was unfortunate because the original bridges built by the engineer, William Chapman, were skew bridges crossing the canal at an angle. The techniques for building humpbacked skew bridges, which involved complicated lines in the courses of the stonework, had been worked out by the Romans, but Chapman's Naas Canal bridges were the first examples of this type of bridge in these islands. Some traces of the old abutments can still be seen. A feature of Chapman's lock design was the introduction of land racks with the water discharging into the lock from beneath the upper cill.

The old canal store at **Naas Harbour** (now used by a local youth group) and the Earl of Mayo's fine Market House nearby, built in 1813, are an indication of the thriving trade which existed in the past. A passenger boat also operated on this line for a period. Traffic declined from the turn of the century. Reeve's Mill and Maltings at Athgarvan ceased to use the Corbally Extension but Odlum's Mills, which date back to 1790, continued to operate its own fleet of boats on the canal until the 1940s and accepted CIE's decision to withdraw the commercial boats with reluctance. The canal was officially closed to navigation in 1961 but pressure to have it restored began in the 1970s.

Restoration

The re-opening of the branch from **Soldier's Island** to **Naas** in 1987 was the first major restoration project undertaken by The Office of Public Works following the transfer of the canals from CIE. The five locks are now in full working order and the line to **Naas Harbour** is navigable again.

Locks

1	9.3 ft rise	Martin Fogarty based at 15th lock, Main Line Tel: (045) 896 300
2	9.5 ft rise	
3	9.3 ft rise	
4	9.2 ft rise	
5	7.3 ft rise	

Facilities **All Services:** Naas.

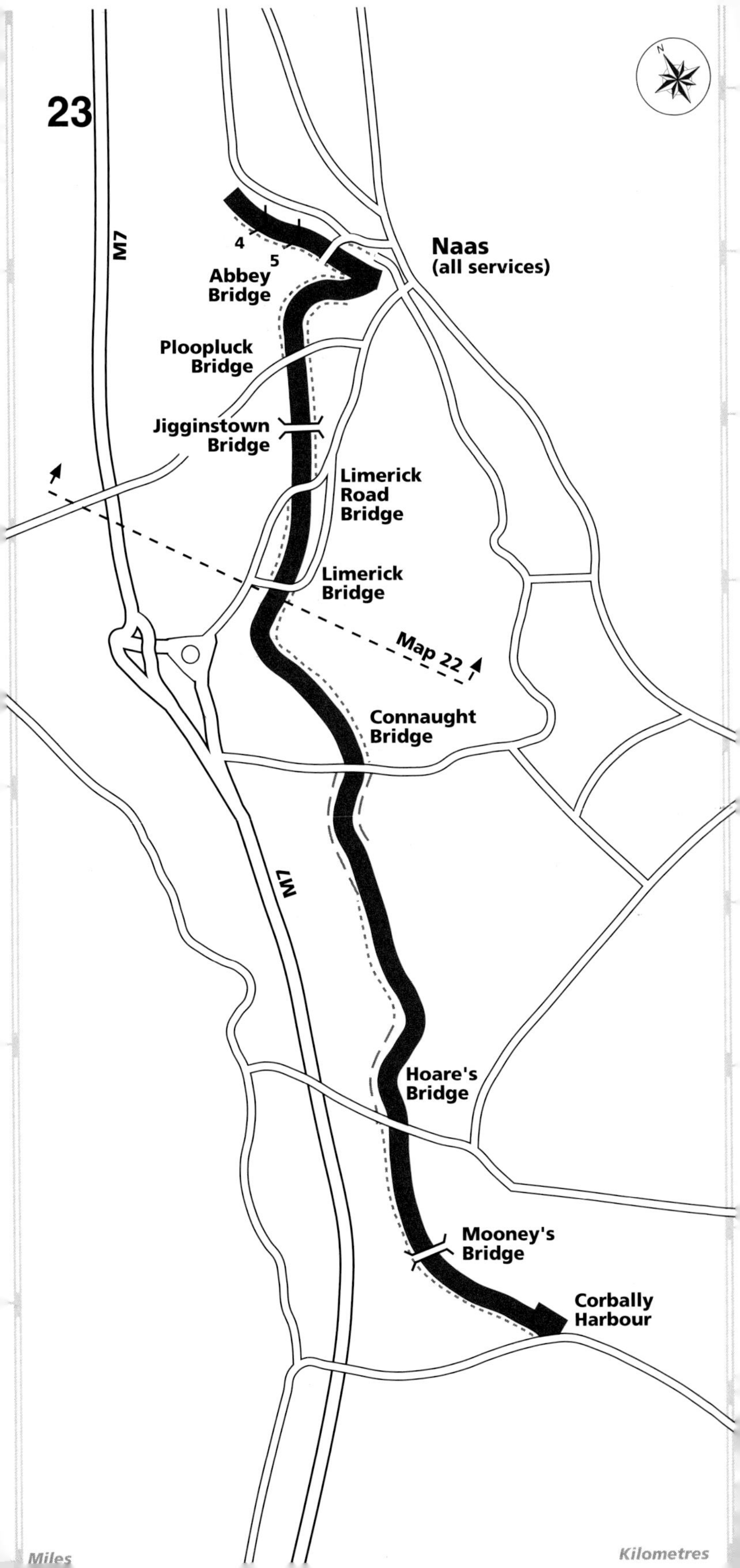
23
M7
4
5
Naas
(all services)
Abbey
Bridge
Plooopluck
Bridge
Jigginstown
Bridge
Limerick
Road
Bridge
Limerick
Bridge
Map 22
Connaught
Bridge
M7
Hoare's
Bridge
Mooney's
Bridge
Corbally
Harbour
Miles
Kilometres

The Naas and Corbally Branch
Naas Harbour to Corbally Harbour

23

The Corbally Extension of the Naas Branch is 5 miles (8 km) long, without any locks. A low level bridge just outside **Naas,** built in the early 1950s, prevents boats from travelling west to **Corbally Harbour**, and makes it unlikely that the branch will ever be restored to navigation. However the banks offer an interesting walk from Naas Harbour to Corbally for the hardy walker, although they can become very wet in winter and overgrown in summer. Walkers must come prepared to negotiate fences across the path, and should be aware of the proximity of cattle in open fields adjoining the canal banks.

The channel, unlike many of the disused branches, has not been allowed to dry out, and supports a wide variety of aquatic plants. The reason the channel remains in water is because the water supply for the entire Naas and Corbally Branch enters the canal at **Corbally Harbour,** and flows from there to **Naas** and then down through the five falling locks to the Main Line at **Soldier's Island.**

History

When the Grand Canal Company bought the canal after the Kildare Canal Company went bankrupt, extensive repairs had to be carried out to make the structures conform with those on the Grand Canal itself. Between 1808 and 1810 the branch line was extended to Corbally where the ruins of old canal buildings can still be seen. However, plans to extend it into Co. Wicklow were abandoned, even though John Killaly did survey a route through Kilcullen and Baltinglas.

The Corbally Extension was built not by an individual contractor, or even by a number of contractors working simultaneously, which had been the way canals were built up until then. It was the first contract undertaken by the civil engineering firm of Henry, Mullins & McMahon (see page 41).

The ruins of Jigginstown House and sixteenth century Castle Rag near the low level bridge on the Corbally Extension are well worth a visit. Jigginstown was a grand mansion built for the Lord Deputy, Thomas Wentworth, Earl of Strafford, in about 1637 to entertain his monarch, Charles I, and for use as a country residence for the Lord Deputy. It was never completed but it remains a fine example of early architecture and brick work.

Facilities

All Services: Naas.

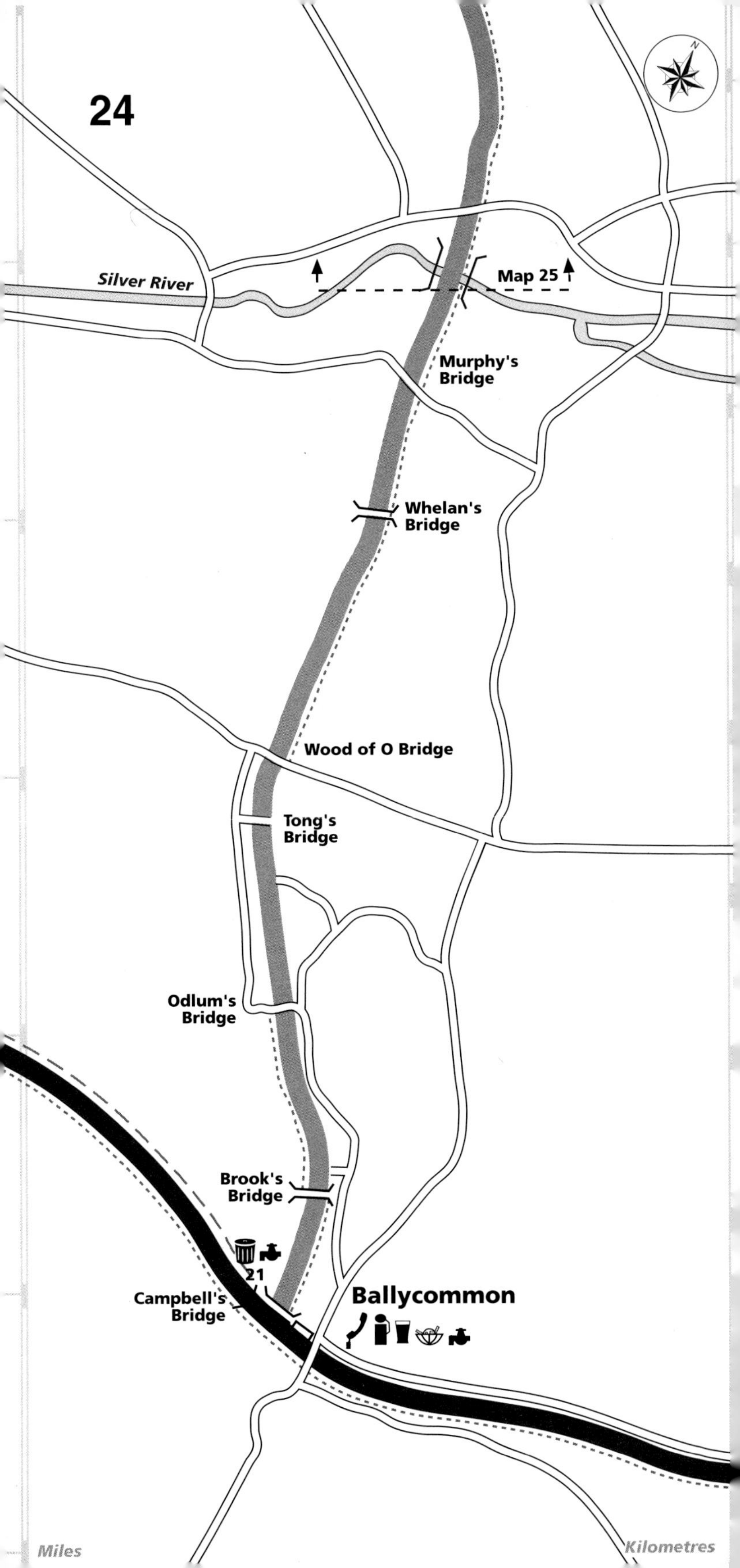
24
Silver River
Map 25
Murphy's Bridge
Whelan's Bridge
Wood of O Bridge
Tong's Bridge
Odlum's Bridge
Brook's Bridge
21
Campbell's Bridge
Ballycommon
Miles
Kilometres

The Kilbeggan Branch
Campbell's Bridge to Murphy's Bridge

24

The Kilbeggan Branch enters the Main Line of the canal at **Ballycommon,** between Daingean and Tullamore (Map 10). There are no locks on the Kilbeggan Branch. A dam was built across the mouth of the branch when it was closed to navigation in 1961, and it was allowed to dry out.

It is possible to walk from **Ballycommon** to **Kilbeggan** along the banks of the disused canal - a distance of 8 miles (13 km) through scrub and grassland, across a raised bog and past esker ridges (mounds of sand and gravel left by the retreating glaciers after the last Ice Age). The paths can be overgrown in summer and very wet in winter, but for the hardy walker they offer an interesting walk with a wide range of scenery. All walkers should come prepared for the following:

- be aware of the proximity of cattle in the open fields adjoining the canal banks;
- come prepared to negotiate any fences you may find across the towpath;
- remember that conditions are likely to be muddy and wet, and that the route is not sign-posted.

History The idea of building a canal to **Kilbeggan** was put forward in 1796. In spite of being invited to do so by a group of local landowners, the Grand Canal Company did not feel that building this branch was a sound business proposition. In 1806 it was suggested that a narrow canal should be built instead. The Grand Canal Company offered to pay the difference in cost if the new canal were built to conform with the existing line, but nothing was done this time either. In 1827, encouraged by its success in getting loans to finance other branches, the Grand Canal Company applied for a loan to build a canal to Kilbeggan. The loan was approved, but the Royal Canal Company lodged a complaint that the new canal would interfere with its trade. The loan approval was withdrawn, but authorised again in 1828, after extensive negotiations. Work on the canal began in 1830.

Facilities **Shop, Garage, Pub, Telephone, Water:**
Ballycommon Bridge.

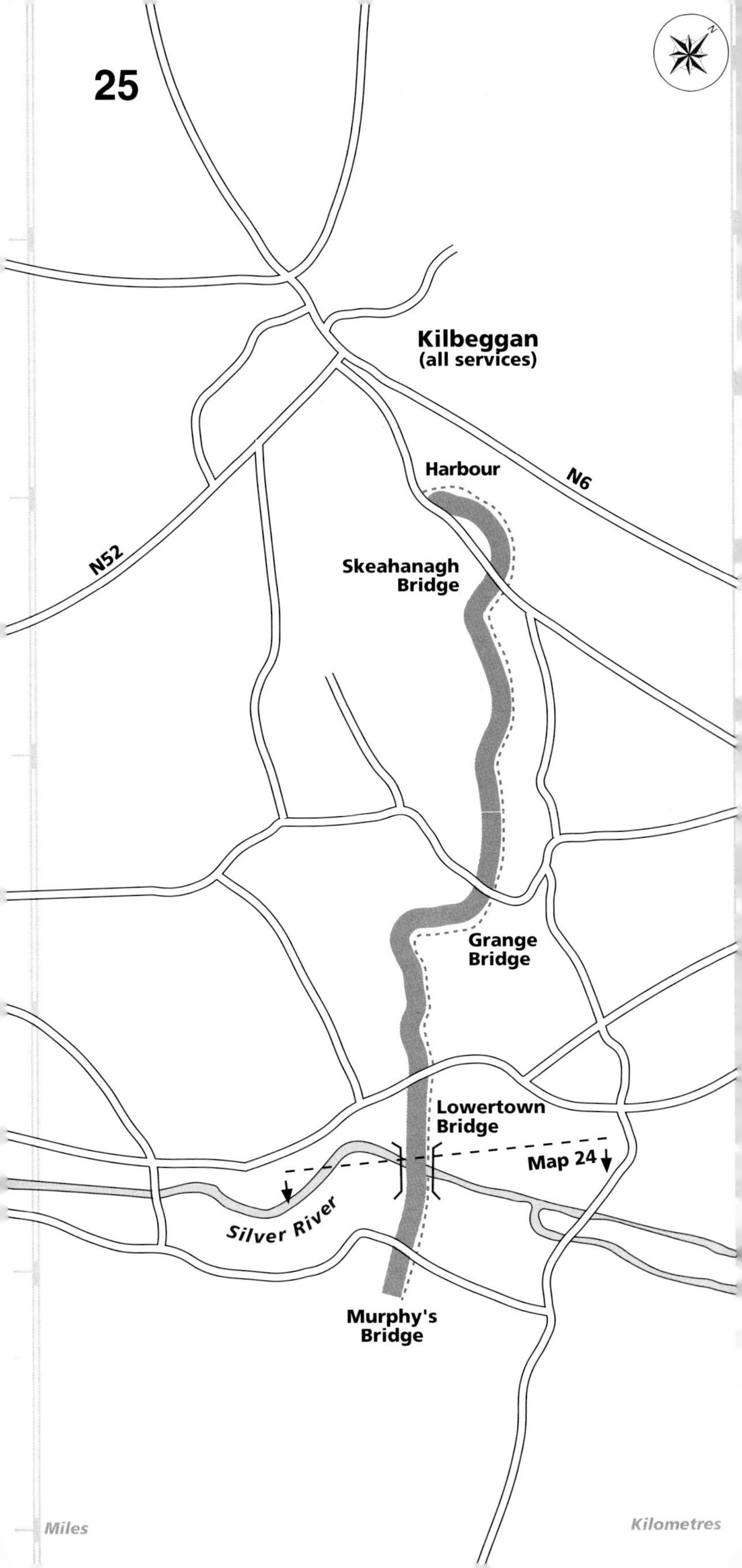
25
Kilbeggan
(all services)
Harbour
N6
N52
Skeahanagh
Bridge
Grange
Bridge
Lowertown
Bridge
Map 24
Silver River
Murphy's
Bridge
Miles
Kilometres

The Kilbeggan Branch
Murphy's Bridge to Kilbeggan Harbour

25

The harbour buildings in **Kilbeggan** were restored in the early 1990s as part of a FÁS scheme by a local group. This was an enormous undertaking as the buildings were in a very derelict condition at that time. The buildings are now used as office premises. The harbour was dredged by The Office of Public Works at the same time. However no feeder streams enter the Kilbeggan Branch, which has to be fed from the Main Line, and so the harbour is still dry.

The wildlife of the **Kilbeggan Branch** is very diverse. The channel was cut through a number of eskers and also crosses a raised bog. An esker is a ridge of sand and gravel left behind by the retreating glaciers after the last Ice Age. Plants growing on eskers have to be tolerant of very calcareous or lime-rich conditions. On raised bogs the soil is very acidic and a different range of plants can be found. When the canal was being built across the bog, lime-rich soil was brought in to build up the towpath. As a result lime-loving plants such as Quaking Grass and Carline Thistle can now be found growing beside acid-loving species such as Purple Moor-grass and Bog Asphodel. However, the paths can be overgrown in summer and very wet in winter, but for the hardy walker they offer an interesting walk with a wide range of scenery. All walkers should come prepared for the following:

- be aware of the proximity of cattle in the open fields adjoining the canal banks;
- come prepared to negotiate any fences you may find across the towpath;
- remember that conditions are likely to be muddy and wet,and that the route is not sign-posted.

History

The contractor who built the Kilbeggan Branch of the Grand Canal was William Dargan, who had just taken over the contract for the construction of the Ulster Canal which was being built at the same time. Dargan, a native of Carlow, had trained as an engineer and surveyor under Thomas Telford on the Holyhead Road. He went on to become one of Ireland's foremost railway engineers, involved in almost every railway built in the country, including the first, the Dublin and Kingstown Railway which opened in December 1834. There is a statue of Dargan in front of the National Gallery of Ireland on Merrion Square in Dublin.

William Dargan was, according to his contract, supposed to complete the canal in one year. In fact it was not opened to traffic until January 1835, four and a half years after work began. Even then the depth of water was still not satisfactory, and Dargan had to continue to maintain and improve the canal until February 1836. The delays were caused largely by problems in staunching the embankments on either side of the **Silver River aqueduct,** on the Offaly and Westmeath county boundary.

Facilities

All Services: Kilbeggan

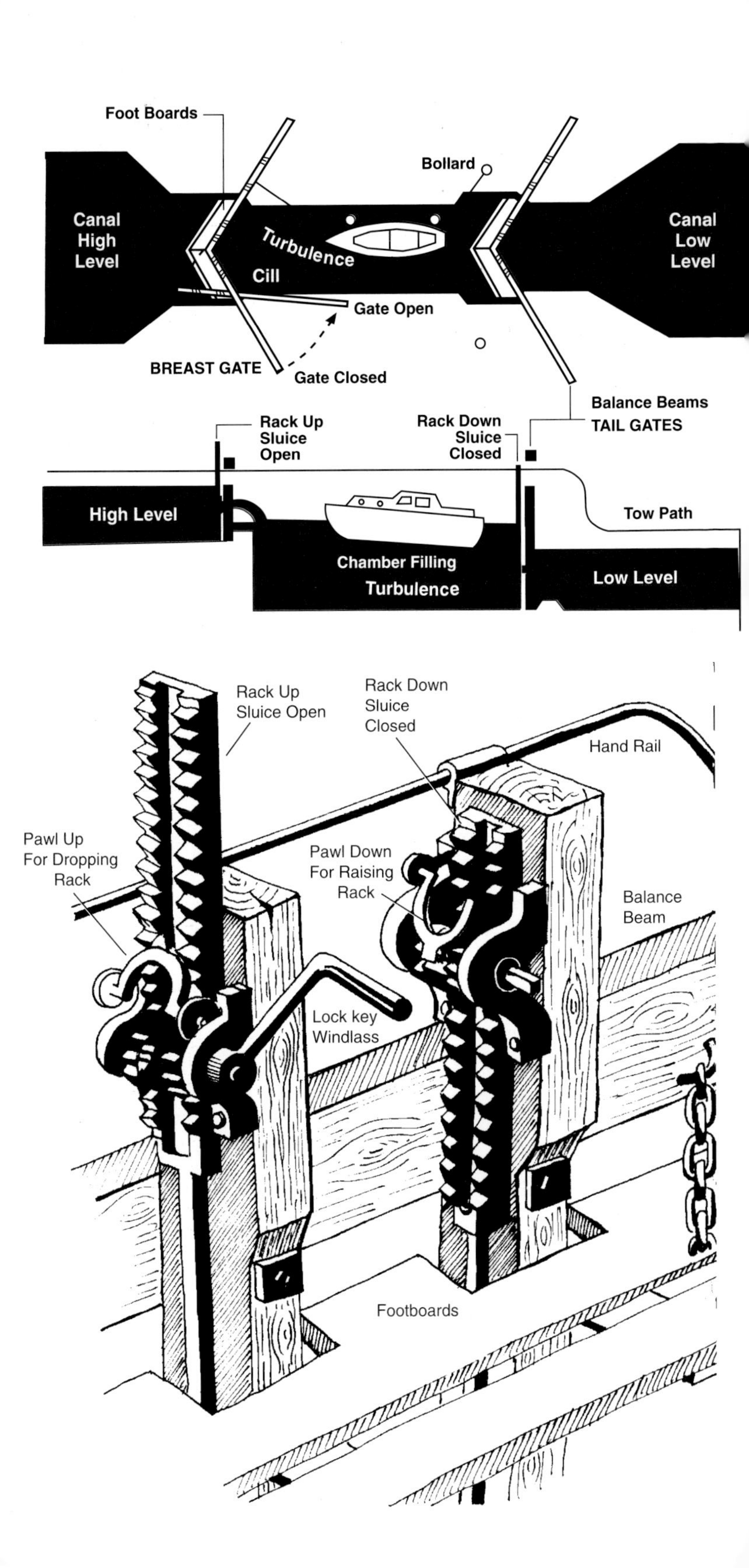
Foot Boards
Bollard
Canal
High
Level
Turbulence
Cill
Canal
Low
Level
Gate Open
BREAST GATE
Gate Closed
Balance Beams
TAIL GATES
Rack Up
Sluice
Open
Rack Down
Sluice
Closed
High Level
Tow Path
Chamber Filling
Turbulence
Low Level
Rack Up
Sluice Open
Rack Down
Sluice
Closed
Hand Rail
Pawl Up
For Dropping
Rack
Pawl Down
For Raising
Rack
Balance
Beam
Lock key
Windlass
Footboards

LOCKS

Lock-keepers live at or near the locks against which their names appear and attend the locks indicated by their brackets. Overlapping duties mean that one lock-keeper attends the 'down' boats and the other the 'up' ones and they share weekend duties. However work practices are under review, and this situation may change in the future.

The inexperienced should use lock gear extremely cautiously: nothing should be done unless you understand the consequences. In good order, lock racks and gates do not need much force to operate.

Keys It is useful but not necessary to carry your own lock key. It is a crank about 18 ins long with a handle at right angles not less than 10 ins long. A hole 1.25 ins square with sides parallel to the handle will fit all rack spindles. Lock keys can be purchased from ***Dúchas* The Heritage Service.**

Descending Fill the chamber by lowering the tail gate racks and then raising those on the breast gates. When full, open the breast gates and move the boat in. A simple ratchet prevents the rack falling when raised but if this is worn, or the pawl is missing, a pebble will do the job. Remove the key. If the ratchet should slip the key would be flung off with some velocity.

Close the breast gates, ensuring that the mitred edges meet cleanly. Close the breast racks and open the tail racks, after ensuring that ropes are not tied but looped or hand held and that no part of the boat can catch on a projection as it falls. Particularly keep the rudder clear of the breast gates and of the cill under them.

Ascending Empty the lock chamber (as for descending), enter, close the tail gates properly after you and lower their racks. Ensure that the boat is well secured bow and stern, with crew ready to shorten the lines as the boat rises. Crew should also watch that no part of the boat is caught under any projection. There is some turbulence when the first breast rack is raised, and the boat will tend to surge forward. It is best to raise the land rack first (if any) or the rack on the same side as the boat is tied, so that the surge of water does not tend to push the boat from wall. Only when the turbulence eases off should a second rack be opened.

Leaving Lock Leave all locks as you found them. Unless another boat is about to use the lock it is usual to leave it empty, with a tail rack up, the breast gates closed and all breast racks down.

Difficulties Gates may jam with rubbish under them or fail to open completely due to rubbish lodging behind them. Re-opening or closing may help, and most lock-keepers have long rakes for dislodging flotsam.

Man Overboard Drop all racks at once and make the rescue from the boat. There are no ladders in the lock chambers.

Courtesy While 'first come first served' is the rule, it is foolish to refuse first passage to a boat coming down if the lock is still full, or vice versa. The lock-keeper is in charge. Offer to help him, but do not hurry him. Enter and leave locks slowly.

FISHING NOTES ON THE GRAND CANAL

A fish stocking programme initiated in 1990 aimed at upgrading the fishing potential of the canals and turning them into a top class coarse fishery. This has involved fish assessment to quantify existing stocks, tagging fish to determine movement patterns and identifying surplus fish from other sources and transferring these to the canals. A research programme was also set up to maintain water quality, with samples taken regularly, and a programme to control weed growth in the water channel. The result of these efforts has been to dramatically improve the fishing potential of the canal.

This has led to a noticeable increase in the number of organised fishing competitions and in the level of foreign anglers using the canals. Most especially, there has been a significant growth in the number of local residents who fish the canal individually and this is an aspect which ***Dúchas* The Heritage Service** is particularly keen to encourage.

The Grand Canal holds large stocks of Bream, Roach, Rudd, various hybrids, Tench, Perch, Pike and Eels.

SEE ILLUSTRATIONS ON INSIDE BACK COVER.

Bream A shoal fish, they grow on the canal to 6lbs (2.7kg). They are caught mostly on small red worm or maggot. They can be located by looking at a stretch on a calm evening and detecting the bubbles which they send to the surface. Very light ground-baiting is important to hold the fish in one area. Bream frighten easily in the canal and minimum bank noise is essential if one is to have success.

Rudd These are a lovely golden coloured fish with red fins. A shy fish, they are caught on maggot or bread flake, i.e. fresh bread, lightly pinched on to a small hook. Rudd can be held in one area by throwing light ground-bait loosely into the water. When one has caught a few fish, they will often move away. They fish best in the evening near dusk.

Roach These fish resemble Rudd but have slightly red fins and a body with a silver-purple tinge . They are prolific breeders and can over-run a system quickly, often resulting in the reduction in size of other species. They feed freely over the whole year and take maggot baits.

Pike Some Pike to 20lbs (9kg) have been taken on the Canal but one is more likely to catch fish of 3 to 6lbs (1.4 - 2.7kg). These fish, common throughout the country, will take a spinning bait, such as a spoon or plug.

Perch A common fish which take worm or maggot or even a spinning bait. They are mostly small in the Canal.

Tench A fine scaled fish, brown in colour and with red eyes. A great fighting fish, they grow to specimen size of 6lbs (2.7kg) and are taken mostly in the evening and early morning with bread, red worm or sweet corn as bait.

Carp These are a specialist's fish and are not easily caught by the average angler. They are shy and often require extreme patience to catch, with the angler using such strange baits as sausage or meat.

Techniques for Canal Angling

The canal is shallow and in some stretches where the water is clear, angling is difficult during daylight. Extreme caution must be taken to avoid noise or bank disturbance as the fish will detect every move because there is little cover. Light tackle, i.e. line and hooks, is essential for success on the canal.

When anglers are seen on the bank, boat-users should remember that boat movement will undoubtedly destroy their sport for at least one or two hours. So please travel slowly by anglers.

ECOLOGY AND WILDLIFE OF THE GRAND CANAL

Summit-level canals like the Grand Canal are man-made waterways which cut across watersheds, linking rivers which would otherwise remain isolated. They act as corridors along which wildlife can travel, on land and in the water.

The vegetation along the Grand Canal has changed and developed in the two hundred years since it was built. The ecological variation found today depends on the level of use of both the water channel and the towpath, on the surrounding natural vegetation, and on the degree of management carried out now and in the past. Without maintenance a canal would silt up, the towpath would become overgrown, and its wildlife interest would be lost.

Deep Water

Milfoils and pondweeds grow in the deep water of the central channel. A range of tiny invertebrates such as snails and insect larvae live on and in the clumps of vegetation. These plants and the insects they support are at the bottom of a complex food chain, and are the food supply for the higher levels including larger invertebrates, coarse fish and birds.

Reed Fringe

The reed fringe grows in the shallow water at the edge of the canal. It is dominated by grasslike plants including reeds and sedges, but includes other wild flowers such as Bogbean, Greater and Lesser Spearwort and Marsh Marigold. The reed fringe acts as a protective buffer, dispersing wave energy generated by wind and boats, and thus helping to prevent bank erosion.

It also helps to maintain the health of the waterway, as the growing plants use up excess nutrients which might otherwise encourage algal growth. It provides food and shelter for waterfowl (such as Moorhen), for fish (including Pike) and for a range of tiny invertebrates. Damselflies and dragonflies hover above the reed ringe in summer. Their larvae spend the early part of their lives underwater and crawl up the emergent plants to shed their skin and fly away as adults.

Bank

The canal bank, lying between the channel and the towpath, is a transitional zone between land and water. Plants which can tolerate damp soil are found here -Yellow Iris and Cuckooflower are typical bank species. Other plants on the bank include Marsh Orchids,Common Valerian, the heavily-scented Meadowsweet and Hemp Agrimony. The caterpillars of the Orange-tip Butterfly feed on the Cuckooflower and related species.

Grassland

Grassland is a common habitat along the canal. The different grass and wildflower species found in a grass sward depend on the underlying soil and on the management regime carried out. Grasslands cannot survive without some form of management, usually cutting. Cutting only two or three times a year encourages the development of a colourful meadow, full of wildflowers and many different grass species. A late cut ensures that all plants, grasses as well as wildflowers, have time to flower and set seed before they are mown.

Boundary Hedgerows and Scrub

The hedgerows and scrub along the canal boundaries provide valuable habitats for wildlife. Birds and small mammals are attracted by the plentiful food supply. In addition to the more obvious sources - fruit, nuts, seeds, berries and nectar - there are many different invertebrates to feed on. Hawthorn, the most common hedge plant, supports over a hundred insect species. The butterflies and moths and their caterpillars are the most conspicuous invertebrates. Larger mammals such as Otters take cover in the dense scrub at the water's edge.

Spring is the best time to see the flowers of the hedge. The white blooms of the Blackthorn appear before the leaves. These are followed by the white flowers of the Hawthorn and Elder. The ground layer plants including Primroses and Celandines also flower in spring, taking advantage of the higher light levels that exist before the shrubs and trees above them come into full leaf.

Stonework

The stonework of locks and bridges provides a series of highly specialised habitats, many of them quite inhospitable. Only lichens can grow on very dry, south-facing walls. Mosses, ferns and other typical wall plants - Rustyback Fern, Wall-rue, Maidenhair Spleenwort, White Stonecrop and Ivy-leaved Toadflax - can survive in damper crevices and on north-facing areas.

Other Habitats

As the canal cuts across the countryside it passes through a variety of habitats - raised bogs, fens, eskers and solid limestone rock. The vegetation of the canal boundary verge (the strip of land between the towpath and the boundary) is influenced by these features.

In the Midlands acid-loving bog plants can be found growing beside the lime-loving plants of the towpaths and canal banks. This botanical contrast is due to the fact that limestone soil was brought in from outside the area to build up the banks when the canal was being constructed through the bog.

The vegetation associated with eskers and rock cuttings is also characterised by lime-loving, low productivity plants such as Carline Thistle and Pyramidal Orchid. The Common Blue Butterfly is found in this habitat.

Conservation

***Dúchas* The Heritage Service** is committed to maximising the amenity potential of the canal, catering for the needs of boaters, anglers, walkers and wildlife enthusiasts. To this end, the maintenance of the Grand Canal is being carried out in a sensitive and balanced manner, taking account of the canal's importance as an environmental resource as well as engineering requirements and the needs of the different recreational users.

Chronological History of the Grand Canal

1751 Establishment of Commissioners of Inland Navigation.

1756 Work commenced on the Grand Canal Scheme.

1763 Thomas Omer, engineer, reported three locks and 10 miles of canal dug from Clondalkin westward.

1765 Dublin Corporation took over the completion of the canal to the Morrell in order to obtain a water supply.

1772 The Company of the Undertakers of the Grand Canal incorporated.

1773 Foundation stone of 1st lock laid by Earl Harcourt and work began on the city sections.

1777 Water supply from the River Morrell to the City Basin near James's Street commenced.

1779 Canal opened to traffic to Sallins.

1780 First passage boat began to ply to Sallins.

1784 Passage boat service extended to Robertstown.

1785 Barrow Line completed to Monasterevin.

1789 Kildare Canal Company completed a branch canal to Naas.

1790 Work began on the Circular Line and it was completed to Portobello.

1791 Barrow Line to Athy completed.

1796 Ringsend Docks completed.

1797 Main Line completed to Daingean (Philipstown).

1798 Main Line completed to Tullamore.

1803 Canal completed to the Shannon but staunching problems delayed the opening.

1804 First trade boat passed through the canal from the Shannon.

1808 Grand Canal Company purchased the Naas Branch.

1810 Naas Branch completed to Corbally.

1824 Work began on the Ballinasloe Branch.

1827 Work began on the Mountmellick Branch.

1828 Ballinasloe Branch opened to traffic.

1830 Work began on the Kilbeggan Branch.

1831 Mountmellick Branch opened to traffic.

1834 Fast fly boats commenced.

1835 Kilbeggan Branch opened to traffic.

1852 Last of the passenger boats withdrawn.

1950 Grand Canal Company merged with Coras Iompair Eireann.

1960 CIE withdrew the trade boats.

1961 Ballinasloe, Mountmellick, Kilbeggan and Naas Branches officially closed to navigation.

1974 James's Street Harbour closed to navigation.

1986 Grand Canal system transferred to The Office of Public Works.

1987 Naas Branch re-opened to Naas Harbour.

1996 Grand Canal system transferred to the Department of Arts, Culture and the Gaeltacht, now the Department of Arts, Heritage, Gaeltacht and the Islands.

DISTANCE TABLE - MAIN LINE

	mile	kilometres
Westmoreland sea lock, Ringsend	0.0	0.0
McMahon Bridge, Ringsend	0.4	0.6
Maquay Bridge & Lock, Grand Canal St.	0.8	1.2
McKenny Bridge & Lock, Lr. Mount St.	0.9	1.4
Huband Bridge & Lock, Up. Mount St.	1.0	1.6
Macartney Bridge & Lock, Baggot St.	1.3	2.0
Eustace Bridge & Lock, Leeson St.	1.6	2.6
Charlemont Bridge & Lock	2.0	3.2
La Touche Bridge & Lock, Portobello	2.3	3.6
Emmet Bridge, Harold's Cross	2.6	4.2
Parnell Bridge	2.9	4.6
Camac Bridge, Dolphin's Barn	3.1	5.0
Harberton Bridge	3.4	5.4
Griffith Bridge, junction with Main Line, 1st Lock, Suir Road Bridge	3.8	6.0
2nd Lock, Goldenbridge footbridge	4.1	6.6
3rd Lock, Blackhorse Bridge, Inchicore	4.8	7.6
4th Lock	5.0	8.0
5th Lock	5.3	8.4
Kylemore Road Bridge	5.4	8.6
6th Lock	5.5	8.8
7th Lock, Ballyfermot Bridge	6.0	9.6
8th Lock	6.5	10.4
M50 Bridge	7.0	11.2
9th Lock, Clondalkin Bridge	7.6	12.2
10th Lock	7.9	12.6
11th Lock	8.1	13.0
12th Lock, Lucan Road Bridge	10.0	16.0
Gollierstown Bridge	10.9	17.4
Hazlehatch Bridge	12.9	20.6
Aylmer's Bridge	14.0	22.4
13th Lock	14.6	23.4
Henry Bridge	15.4	24.6
Ponsonby Bridge	16.9	27.0
14th Lock, Devonshire Bridge	18.4	29.4
15th Lock	18.8	30.0
Railway Bridge	20.0	32.0
Sallins Bridge	20.8	33.2
Junction with Naas Line	21.3	34.0
Leinster Aqueduct	21.9	35.0
16th Lock, Digby Bridge	23.3	37.2
17th Lock, Landenstown Bridge	23.9	38.2
18th Lock	24.8	39.6
Burgh or Cock Bridge	25.5	40.8
Bonynge or Healy's Bridge	26.6	42.6
Binn's Bridge, Robertstown	28.0	44.8
19th Lock, Lowtown & Lowtown Marina	28.9	46.2
Junction with new Barrow Line	29.0	46.4
Bond Bridge, Allenwood	30.0	48.0
Shee or Scow Bridge	30.9	49.4
Light Railway Bridge (lifting)	31.9	51.0
Hamilton Bridge	33.3	53.2

Bord na Móna Bridge, Kilpatrick	34.0	54.4
Hartley Bridge, Ticknevin	35.4	56.6
20th Lock, Ticknevin	35.9	57.4
Blundell Aqueduct, The Tunnel	38.8	62.0
Downshire Bridge, Edenderry Line	39.9	63.8
Colgan's Bridge	40.1	64.2
George's Bridge	40.3	64.4
Rathmore Bridge	40.8	65.2
Cartland Bridge	41.8	66.8
Trimblestown Bridge	43.0	68.8
Rhode Bridge	45.8	73.2
Toberdaly Bridge	46.4	74.2
Light Railway Bridge (lifting)	47.4	75.8
Killeen Bridge	49.3	78.8
Molesworth Bridge, Daingean	50.9	81.4
Bord na Móna bridge (fixed span)	52.9	84.4
Chenevix Bridge, Ballycommon	54.3	86.8
Campbell's Bridge, over Kilbeggan Line	54.4	87.0
21st Lock, Ballycommon	54.5	87.2
22nd Lock, Cappyroe Bridge	55.4	88.6
23rd Lock	55.8	89.2
24th Lock, Celtic Canal Cruisers	57.6	92.2
25th Lock, Cappincur Bridge	58.0	92.8
26th Lock	58.5	93.6
Bury Bridge, over Tullamore Harbour junction	59.4	95.0
Kilbeggan Road Bridge, Tullamore	59.6	95.4
27th Lock, Cox's Bridge	59.9	95.8
28th Lock	60.1	96.2
New Bridge	60.3	96.4
Railway Bridge	60.4	96.6
Shra Bridge	61.1	97.8
29th Lock, Ballycowan Bridge	62.3	99.6
Huband Aqueduct	62.5	100.0
Charleville Aqueduct	63.1	101.0
Corcoran's Bridge, Rahan.	64.8	103.6
Becan's Bridge, Rahan.	65.5	104.8
Henesy's Bridge	66.1	105.8
30th Lock, Ballincloughin Bridge	66.6	106.6
31st Lock, Cornalour Bridge	67.1	107.4
Plunkett Bridge, Pollagh	69.4	111.0
Light Railway Bridge (swivel)	72.1	115.4
Derry Bridge	72.8	116.4
Macartney Aqueduct, Silver River	74.1	118.6
Armstrong Bridge, Gallen	76.0	121.6
Noggus Bridge	76.4	122.2
32nd Lock, Glyn Bridge	76.9	123.0
Judge's Bridge	77.6	124.2
33rd Lock, Belmont Bridge	78.1	125.0
L'Estrange Bridge	79.8	127.6
34th Lock, Clononey Bridge	80.4	128.6
Griffith Bridge, Shannon Harbour	81.3	130.0
35th Lock	81.6	130.6
36th Lock, junction with Shannon	81.9	131.0

DISTANCE TABLE - BARROW LINE

Distance from junction with Main Line at Lowtown to

	miles	kilometres
Littletown Bridge	0.9	1.4
Ballyteague Bridge	1.8	2.8
20th lock, Ballyteague	2.1	3.4
21st lock, Ballyteague	2.3	3.6
22nd lock, Glenaree Bridge	5.3	8.4
Rathangan Bridge	7.8	12.4
23rd lock, Spencer Bridge and Canalways Ireland	8.3	13.2
Wilson's Bridge	9.6	15.4
Umeras Bridge	11.1	17.8
24th lock, Macartney's Bridge	13.0	20.8
Shepherd's Brook or High Bridge	13.9	22.2
Monasterevin lifting bridge and Barrow Aqueduct	14.4	23.0
Junction with Mountmellick Branch	14.5	23.2
25th lock, Moore's Bridge	14.6	23.4
Clogheen Bridge, Dublin Road	15.0	24.0
Old Bridge	16.5	26.4
Fisherstown Bridge	18.3	29.2
Courtwood Bridge	19.4	31.0
Grattan Aqueduct	20.4	32.6
Vicarstown Bridge, Vicarstown Leisure Barges	21.8	34.8
Camac Aqueduct	22.6	36.2
Ballymanus Bridge	23.0	36.8
Milltown Bridge	25.6	41.0
26th lock, Cardington Bridge	27.8	44.4
Lennon's Bridge	27.9	44.6
27th lock, Athy and Augustus Bridge	28.3	45.2
28th lock, junction with River Barrow	28.5	45.6

DISTANCE TABLE - KILBEGGAN BRANCH

Distance from junction with Main Line at Ballycommon to

	miles	kilometres
Campbell's Bridge	0.0	0.0
Brook's Bridge	0.6	1.0
Odlum's Bridge	1.4	2.2
Tong's Bridge	2.2	3.5
Wood of O Bridge	2.5	4.0
Whelan's Bridge	3.8	6.1
Murphy's Bridge	4.3	6.9
Lowertown Bridge	5.1	8.2
Grange Bridge	6.3	10.1
Skeahanagh Bridge	7.8	12.5
Kilbeggan Harbour	8.2	13.1

DúCHAS THE HERITAGE SERVICE

Dúchas* The Heritage Service** is part of the Department of Arts, Heritage, Gaeltacht and the Islands. It is the State body responsible for the protection and conservation of Ireland's natural and built heritage. The maintenance and development of an extensive network of inland waterways as a major recreational amenity forms just part of the duties of the organisation. ***Dúchas owns and manages National Parks and nature reserves, as well as actively encouraging citizens to protect wildlife in areas outside State care. ***Dúchas*** is also entrusted with the conservation of Ireland's archaeological and architectural heritage - from prehistoric burial sites and monastic settlements to Norman castles and historic houses.

Ireland's inland waterways, built or improved in the 18th and 19th centuries for commercial transport, are today used for a variety of recreational pursuits - boating (of course!) in a range of large and small boats, fishing, and walking - and are enjoyed by all who appreciate nature, local history and industrial archaeology.

Grand Canal

When responsibility for the Grand Canal (with the Barrow Navigation and the Royal Canal) was transferred to the State in 1986, the fabric of the system was in very poor condition. Since then considerable effort has been made in upgrading the canal. Major repairs have been carried out to the bog embankments to safeguard these sections. Most lock gates have now been replaced and deep gate jetties installed, dredging has been undertaken, moorings provided, water supplies augmented and weed control greatly improved.

The canal is more than just a boating amenity, and facilities for non-boaters are also being developed. Walking routes have been opened and sign-posted along the towpath. Water quality is now regularly monitored, and a major fish-stocking programme is being carried out. An ecological survey was carried out, and nature conservation principles have been incorporated into maintenance works. The public amenity role of the canal is promoted and protected at all times.

Barrow Navigation

Widely considered to be the most picturesque of all Irish waterways, the Barrow Navigation is being upgraded by ***Dúchas* The Heritage Service.** Ongoing works include the replacement of lock gates, dredging of the boat channel and canal cuts, provision of slips and mooring facilities, and making the towpath more accessible for walkers. A companion volume to this guide, ***A Guide to the Barrow Navigation,*** is available.

Royal Canal

The Royal Canal was closed to navigation in 1961. Over the years the canal dried up; channel, banks and towpath were lost under a tangle of vegetation; and low bridges were built over the once-busy waterway. Restoration of the canal, initiated by the Inland Waterways Association of Ireland and the Royal Canal Amenity Group, has been carried on by the State since 1987. The canal is being developed for more than just boating - the heavily overgrown towpath is being opened up for walkers; and a fisheries development programme is being carried out. The public amenity role of the canal is promoted and protected at all times. ***A Guide to the Royal Canal*** is also available.

Shannon Navigation

The Shannon Navigation has been the responsibility of the State since the middle of the last century. Over the last three decades facilities for boating traffic have been greatly improved with the provision of new quays, jetties and harbours; upgrading of the locks; and the opening of new destinations (Lough Allen via the Lough Allen Canal and the Erne Navigation through the Shannon - Erne Waterway). Further extensions are being planned and executed, including the construction of a new navigation on the River Suck to Ballinasloe. Navigation charts for the Shannon Navigation are available.

Shannon - Erne Waterway

The link between the Shannon and the Erne (formerly called the Ballinamore & Ballyconnell Canal) was re-opened in 1994 following over a century of dereliction. In that year over 3,000 boats passed along the restored waterway - two hundred times more than used it during the nine years that it was opened for commercial traffic (1860-69). Navigation charts for this waterway have been published.

THE INLAND WATERWAYS ASSOCIATION OF IRELAND

IWAI was formed in 1954 to promote the development, use and maintenance of Ireland's navigable rivers and canals. When the Shannon was still almost totally undeveloped for pleasure boating, IWAI fought the building of low bridges, thus ensuring the survival of the river as a national tourism asset. Later the Association successfully fought the threatened closure of the Grand Canal in Dublin, which would have cut the Shannon off from the east coast.

Improvement and Restoration

Over the years the IWAI has attracted public interest in the potential of the waterways. It has lobbied successfully for the restoration of access to Lough Allen, the re-opening of the Shannon-Erne Waterway (formerly the Ballinamore and Ballyconnell Canal), and for various other extensions to the network. The Association is currently campaigning for the restoration of the Ulster Canal, which would link the Erne system with Lough Neagh. Individual branches of the IWAI focus attention on local issues in their areas.

Rallies

The Association organises annual rallies on the Grand Canal, Shannon, Barrow, Shannon-Erne Waterway, Corrib, Erne, Nore and Slaney and many other events and festivals. Competitions help to raise standards of boatmanship and seaworthiness.

Social Events

Film shows, lectures and social occasions help to bring together waterways users out of season.

Publications

The Association publishes a newsletter, ***Inland Waterways News,*** which is sent out to every member quarterly and brings local activities and developments into perspective. Some branches produce local newsletters.

The IWAI initiated the series of guide books for the Grand and Royal Canals and Barrow Navigation at a time when there was a great need for such publications. More recently, individual branches have published books of interest, notably the reprint of ***Green and Silver*** and a book on the Shannon-Erne Waterway, both in 1994.

Branches and Membership

The IWAI is made up of the following branches: Athlone, Barrow, Belturbet, Boyne, Carrick-on-Shannon, Corrib, Dublin, Kildare, Lough Derg, Northern Ireland, Offaly, Shannon Harbour and Slaney - all represented on a national council. Details about membership can be obtained by email from the IWAI website at IWAI.ie or from:

IWAI,
Stone Cottage,
Claremont Road,
Killiney,
Co. Dublin.

Typesetting & Maps ERA-Maptec Ltd., 36 Dame Street,
Dublin 2.
Tel: +353-1-679 9227.